OCS Study
MMS 2001-063

I0423554

Spatial and Temporal Variability of Plankton Stocks on the Basis of Acoustic Backscatter Intensity and Direct Measurements in the Northeastern Gulf of Mexico

Final Report

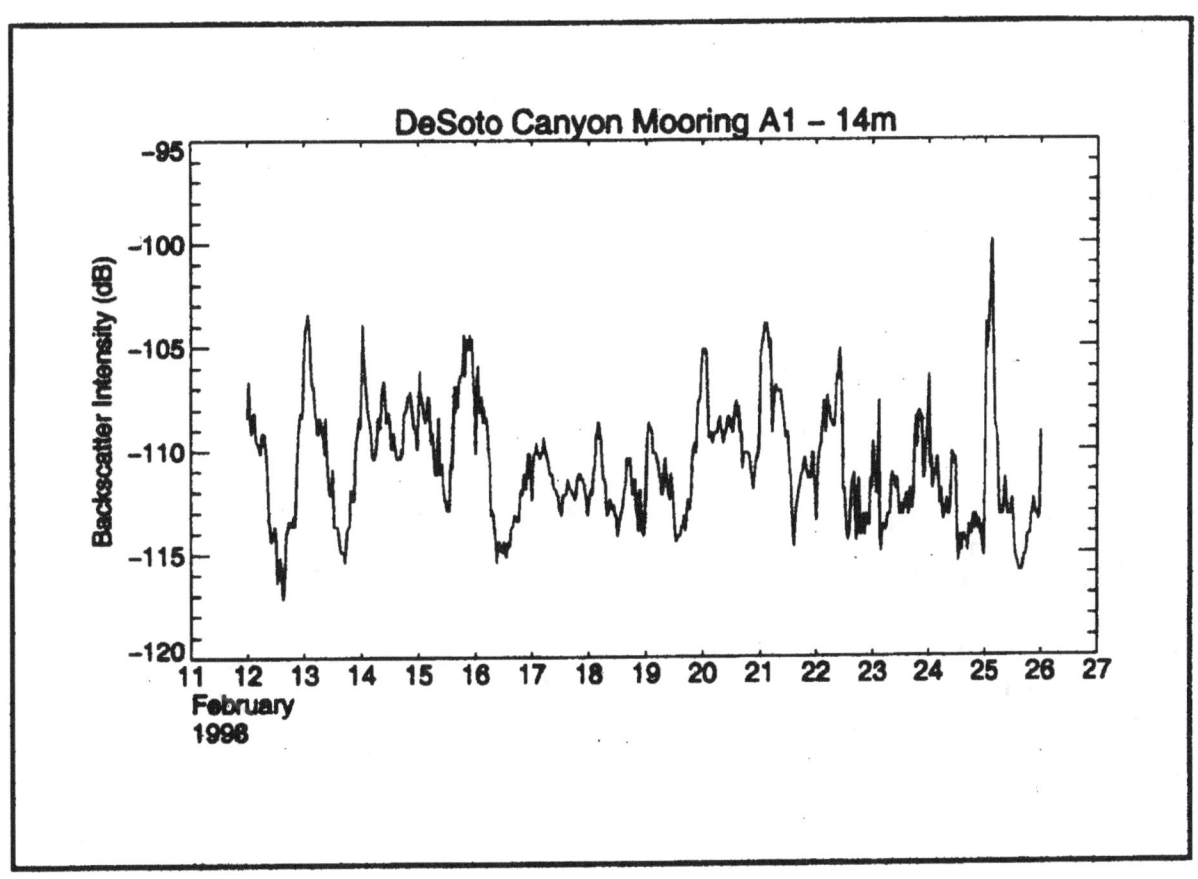

U.S. Department of the Interior
Minerals Management Service
Gulf of Mexico OCS Region

OCS Study
MMS 2001-063

Spatial and Temporal Variability of Plankton Stocks on the Basis of Acoustic Backscatter Intensity and Direct Measurements in the Northeastern Gulf of Mexico

Final Report

Authors

Rebecca L. Scott
Douglas C. Biggs
Steven F. DiMarco

Prepared under MMS Contract
1435-01-97-CA-30851
by
Texas A&M University
Department of Oceanography
College Station, Texas 77843-3146

Published by

U.S. Department of the Interior
Minerals Management Service
Gulf of Mexico OCS Region

New Orleans
August 2001

DISCLAIMER

This report was prepared under contract between the Minerals Management Service (MMS) and the Texas A&M Research Foundation. This report has been technically reviewed by the MMS, and it has been approved for publication. Approval does not signify that the contents necessarily reflect the views and policies of the MMS, nor does the mention of trade names or commercial products constitute endorsement or recommendation for use. It is, however, exempt from review and compliance with the MMS editorial standards.

REPORT AVAILABILITY

Extra copies of the report may be obtained from the Public Information Office (Mail Stop 5034) at the following address:

U.S. Department of the Interior
Minerals Management Service
Gulf of Mexico OCS Region
Public Information Office (MS 5034)
1201 Elmwood Park Boulevard
New Orleans, Louisiana 70123-2394

Telephone: (504) 736-2519 or
1-800-200-GULF

CITATION

Suggested citation:

Scott, R.L., D.C. Biggs, and S.F. DiMarco. 2001. Spatial and Temporal Variability of Plankton Stocks on the Basis of Acoustic Backscatter Intensity and Direct Measurements in the Northeastern Gulf of Mexico. OCS Study MMS 2001-063, U.S. Dept. of the Interior, Minerals Management Service, Gulf of Mexico OCS Region, New Orleans, LA. 117 pp.

ABOUT THE COVER

The cover figure depicts a two-week time series of unfiltered acoustic backscatter intensity (ABI) from near-surface water at mooring A1. The saw tooth alternation of ABI is a consequence of the diel vertical migration of zooplankton out of the near-surface water (day) and back into near-surface water (night). The record runs from full moon (February 12, 1998) to new moon (February 27, 1998).

ACKNOWLEDGMENTS

We gratefully acknowledge Dr. Alexis Lugo-Fernandez (MMS COTR) for supporting this analysis of coupled biological-physical oceanographic data as an add-on option to the primary NEGOM Chemical Oceanography and Hydrography Study (MMS Contract 1435-01-97-CT-30851). This add-on funding supported Ms. Rebecca Scott as a Graduate Research Assistant during the two year period that she worked on data reduction and synthesis for this project (January 1999 - December 2000). The summary and analyses that are presented in this Final Report are the core of the research that Ms. Scott has carried out for her MS thesis of the same title (MS in Oceanography, Texas A&M University, expected August 2001). That thesis will archive additional information to include: (1) detailed taxonomic composition of the zooplankton collections taken on NEGOM cruises 2, 3, 4, and 5; (2) length-frequency information of the crustacean zooplankton in these collections; (3) additional comparison of ADCP backscatter intensity with sea surface chlorophyll fields using SeaWiFS imagery.

We also gratefully acknowledge Dr. Peter Hamilton and Dr. Evans Waddell of Science Applications International Corporation (Raleigh, NC) for providing the ADCP echo intensity data from the 12 upward-looking ADCPs moored as part of the DeSoto Canyon Eddy Intrusion Study (MMS Contract 1435-01-96-CT-30825). We especially appreciate the willingness of these scientists to share data from a study in progress and to allow us to continue and extend their analysis of ADCP current data.

Colleagues at the University of South Florida (USF) contributed to this study by compiling time series of SeaWiFS chlorophyll data at each of the DeSoto Canyon ADCP mooring locations. With guidance from Drs. Frank Muller-Karger and Chuanmin Hu, USF graduate student Andrew Remsen composited all available SeaWiFS imagery from the Gulf of Mexico for 1998 and 1999 into biweekly intervals.

Finally, we thank the Department of Oceanography, Texas A&M University, for the financial support of Ms. Scott during her first semester of study at TAMU (fall 1998). We also thank TAMU and MMS for travel support that Ms. Scott received to present aspects of this research at national scientific meetings of the American Society of Limnology and Oceanography.

ABSTRACT

To investigate the utility of Acoustic Doppler Current Profilers (ADCPs) for estimating the spatial and temporal variability of zooplankton stocks in the northeastern Gulf of Mexico, acoustic data from a moored array of ADCPs were used in conjunction with sea truth zooplankton samples. As part of the DeSoto Canyon Eddy Intrusion Study, twelve Broadband ADCPs were moored along four cross-margin lines in the DeSoto Canyon area of the northeastern Gulf of Mexico. These upward-looking ADCPs were moored at approximately 90-m depth and deployed March 1997 through April 1999. To obtain sea truth for the backscatter data, net tows were made during spring, summer, and fall of 1998 as well as spring 1999.

Results of this combined physical and biological research show that acoustic backscatter intensity data recorded by ADCPs do represent a biological signal that serves as an approximation for zooplankton standing stocks in the northeastern Gulf of Mexico. Spectral analysis of acoustic data reveals daily variability in acoustic backscatter intensity as well as low frequency, weekly to monthly, variability. This low frequency variability in acoustic backscatter intensity is linked to currents in the DeSoto Canyon area, and correlations between acoustic backscatter intensity and current velocity vary with the movement of warm slope eddies and other mesoscale circulation features in the Gulf. Wind mixing associated with hurricane-strength storm events appears to affect the acoustic backscatter recorded by ADCPs, and increases in acoustic backscatter intensity during these periods are attributed to the downward mixing of bubbles from surface turbulence. From this research the interactions between physics and biology are evident, and we recommend that data recorded by moored ADCPs enable investigation of such interactions.

TABLE OF CONTENTS

TABLE OF CONTENTS (continued)

LIST OF FIGURES

xi

LIST OF FIGURES (continued)

LIST OF TABLES

1.0 **Introduction**

1.1 **Background**

Because of their ability to remotely measure current velocity in the water column over a vertical range from a few meters to hundreds of meters, acoustic Doppler current profilers (ADCPs) have become increasingly important constituents of physical oceanographic research since their development in the mid-1980s (Woodward and Appell 1986). Developed from the Doppler speed log that estimated ship speed at the surface relative to speed over the ocean bottom, the ADCP was engineered to measure current speed and direction at multiple depths throughout the water column (Gordon 1996). Shortly after these ADCPs were put into use aboard University-National Oceanographic Laboratory System (UNOLS) research vessels, it was recognized that useful biological data can be extracted from the backscattered acoustic energy of the ADCP while simultaneously measuring current velocity (Flagg and Smith 1989; Smith et al. 1989). The biological use is based on the premise that zooplankton in the water column are the predominant particles that scatter sound pulses transmitted by ADCPs. Thus, the absolute backscatter intensity of the acoustic pulses is thought to represent a biological signal directly related to the size and concentration of zooplankton in the water column (Brierley et al. 1998).

Research conducted by Flagg and Smith (1989) found that there was a correlation between zooplankton volume (measured as ml wet weight / m^3) and the intensity of the ADCP backscattered acoustic signal. ADCPs, therefore, offered an indirect means to census zooplankton (Flagg and Smith 1989). Combined biological and acoustic research began to increase in the early 1990s, and ADCP backscatter intensity has now been used in various research projects to estimate zooplankton abundance (Heywood et al. 1991; Roe and Griffiths 1993; Griffiths and Diaz 1996; Rippeth and Simpson 1998; Zimmerman and Biggs 1999; Wormuth et al. 2000). In fact, the demand for acoustical data in ecological studies is escalating, and the analysis of plankton acoustics has become an increasingly important bridge between physical and biological oceanography.

1.2 **Description of the Study Area**

The Yucatan Channel and the Florida Straits serve as the only two openings to adjacent bodies of water for the semi-enclosed Gulf of Mexico basin. Circulation in the eastern Gulf is dominated by the Yucatan Current, which carries water from the Caribbean Sea into the Gulf of Mexico through the Yucatan Channel. As the Yucatan Current moves northward into the Gulf of Mexico it makes a sharp clockwise turn and becomes known as the Loop Current. As the Loop Current progresses northward into the Gulf, instability leads to the shedding of large rings known as Loop Current Eddies (Hoffman and Worley 1986; Sturges and Leben 2000). These mesoscale circulation features, with radial dimensions on the order of 150 - 250 km, also produce smaller cyclonic (counterclockwise rotating) and anticyclonic (clockwise rotating) eddies found throughout the Gulf. Research suggests that circulation in the western Gulf of Mexico can be dominated by such cyclonic-anticyclonic eddy pairs (Capurro and Reid 1972; Nowlin et al. 2001; Hamilton et al. 2000).

The DeSoto Canyon region of the Gulf of Mexico is located between the Mississippi Delta and the West Florida Shelf. The exchanges of nutrients and organisms between the continental shelf and deep waters in the eastern Gulf of Mexico are affected by circulation patterns in this canyon area and the upper continental slope, and the eddies generated over the northeastern Gulf slope greatly influence transport (Hamilton 1999; Nowlin et al. 2000). The DeSoto Canyon region of the northeastern Gulf of Mexico serves as the study area for this bioacoustic research.

1.3 Study Objectives

As part of the DeSoto Canyon Eddy Intrusion Study (EIS), twelve 300 kHz broadband ADCPs were moored along the slopes of the DeSoto Canyon in the Northeastern Gulf of Mexico. The EIS, funded by the U.S. Department of the Interior, Minerals Management Service (OCS contract 1435-01-CT-30825) monitored the circulation of the DeSoto Canyon area for two years in order to determine the effect of Loop Current eddies over the continental margin of the northeastern Gulf of Mexico. The Workhorse® ADCPs used in the study were manufactured by RD Instruments, Inc. of San Diego, California and deployed by Science Applications International Corporation (SAIC). The twenty-five month mooring deployment period extended March 1997 through April 1999 and consisted of six instrument deployment/re-deployment periods of approximately four months each. During this time the twelve moored ADCPs recorded current velocity as well acoustic backscatter intensity (ABI) data. Table 1.3-1 details the location of each mooring, as well as the total water depth at each mooring and depth of each instrument.

Table 1.3-1.

DeSoto Canyon ADCP mooring locations. Note: Mooring D1 was moored at 99m depth during deployment one, but was redeployed at 80m for the remaining five deployments.

MOORING	LATITUDE °N	LONGITUDE °W	WATER DEPTH (M)	INSTRUMENT DEPTH (M)
A1	29.24	88.49	100	80
A2	29.06	88.39	500	90
A3	28.77	88.27	1300	80
B1	29.34	87.91	100	80
B2	29.21	87.87	500	90
B3	29.07	87.86	1300	80
C1	29.59	87.35	100	80
C2	29.37	87.35	500	90
C3	29.00	87.35	1300	80
D1	30.07	86.84	100	80*
D2	29.33	86.85	500	90
E1	29.70	86.33	100	80

The twelve broadband ADCPs were moored in total water depths of 100m, 500m, and 1300m. Figure 1.3-1 depicts the bathymetry of the DeSoto Canyon area of the northeastern Gulf of Mexico and shows the locations of the 12 moorings. Three ADCPs were placed west of 87°W on each line A, B, and C. The remaining three ADCPs were placed between 87°W and 86°W. A narrowband ADCP was moored at a thirteenth location near the head of the DeSoto Canyon in water depth of 200m. This instrument operated at 153 kHz rather than 300 kHz, and the ABI data recorded by this ADCP were not included in this study.

All ADCPs were moored on the bottom and hung suspended at either 80 m or 90 m below the water's surface. Specifically, ADCPs A1, A3, B1, B3, C1, C3, D1 and E1

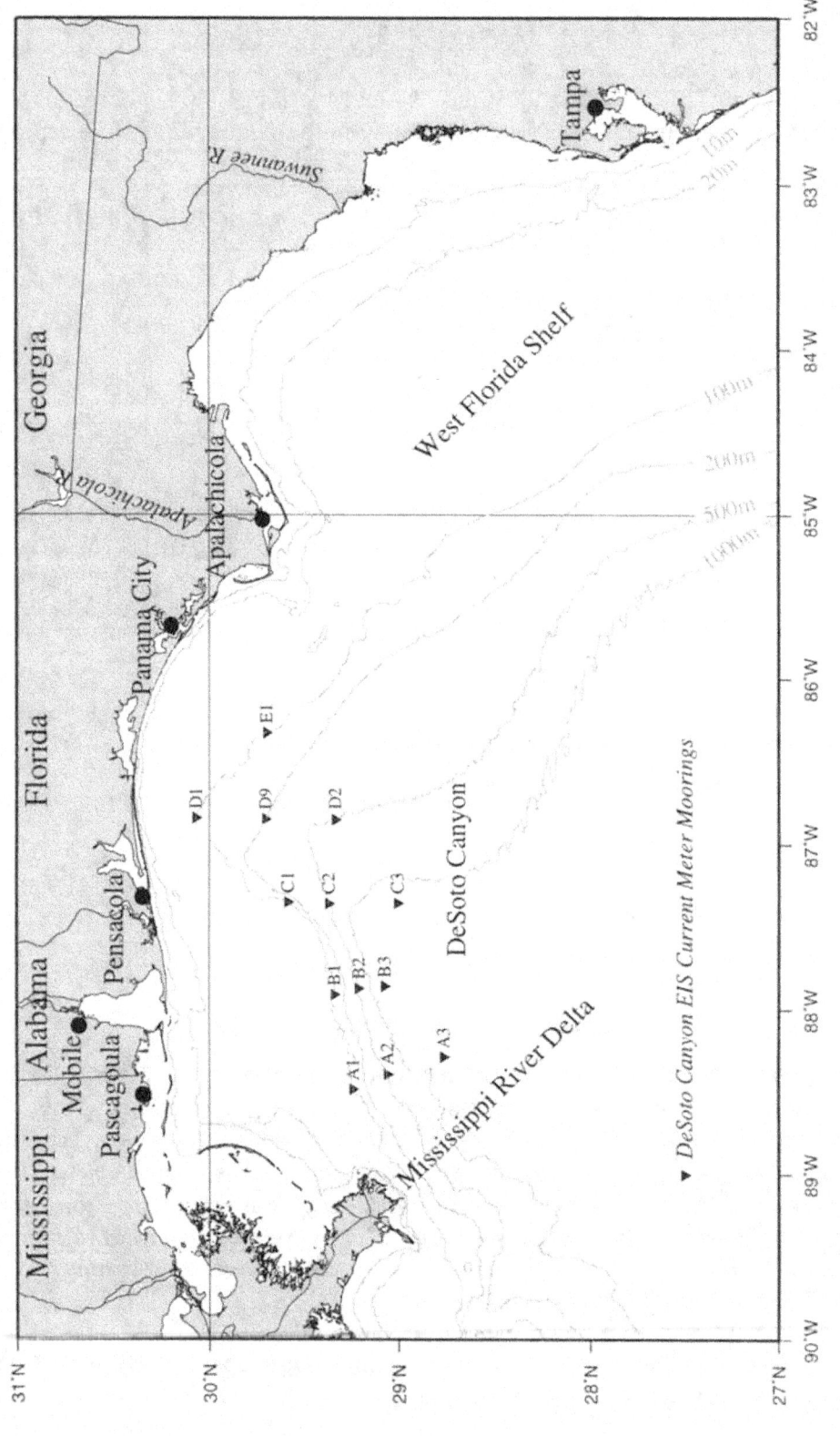

Fig. 1.3-1. Map of the DeSoto Canyon area of the Gulf of Mexico including the location of twelve moored ADCPs.

were suspended 80 m below the surface, while four instruments were suspended 90 m below the surface at total water depths of roughly 500 m (moorings A2, B2, C2 and D2). Each of the twelve ADCPs was moored in an upward-looking orientation and emitted acoustic pulses at a frequency of approximately 300 kHz. Echo intensity data were recorded every 30 minutes during the 25-month mooring deployment period, and these data were recorded in equally spaced 4-meter depth bins. To serve as sea truth for the acoustic backscatter intensity data, zooplankton collections were made on three oceanographic research cruises conducted in the northeastern Gulf during the 25-month ADCP deployment period.

Through analysis of combined acoustic and zooplankton data, this study aimed to determine the utility of ADCPs for recording backscatter intensity data related to the size and concentration of zooplankton in the water column. Furthermore, the use of a moored array of ADCPs for defining spatial and temporal scales of zooplankton stocks in the northeastern Gulf of Mexico was investigated. Past research shows a positive correlation between zooplankton volume and the intensity of the ADCP backscattered signal (Flagg and Smith 1989), and it was expected that the acoustic backscatter intensity data recorded by the 12 moored ADCPs would be valuable in studying the spatial and temporal variability of zooplankton stocks in the northeastern Gulf.

2.0 <u>Methods</u>

2.1 Physical Oceanographic Data Collection

2.1.1 Function of ADCPs

The main feature of the ADCP is its ability to remotely measure current velocity over a range from a few meters to hundreds of meters in the water column. To measure current speed and direction, the ADCP emits high frequency sound pulses and then determines the Doppler shift of the echo that is returned from scatterers in the water column (Emery and Thomson 1997). The Doppler shift is described as the frequency difference between the emitted and reflected sound pulses, and this frequency difference depends on the movement of the scattering particle relative to the emitted sound (Brierley et al. 1998). Zooplankton and micronekton in the water column are the predominant particles that scatter sound pulses emitted by ADCPs, and these particles are assumed to be passive indicators of water motion.

Sound pulses produced by ADCPs are transmitted from an array of four transducers with beams that are oriented at a fixed angle from the axis of the instrument. Trigonometric functions are applied to the current speeds along each of the four beams to produce horizontal and vertical velocity components (Emery and Thomson 1997). The resulting velocity profiles measured by ADCPs are divided into equally spaced segments called depth bins, where each depth bin is analogous to a single current meter. The ADCP thus acts as a stack of individual current meters. While conventional current meters measure currents at one discrete point, the ADCP measures average velocity over the depth range of each depth bin. This averaging of velocity over each depth bin improves the reliability of the measurements (Gordon 1996).

2.1.2 ADCP Data Processing

Because ADCPs can be moored and left unattended for extended time periods, oceanographers are able to collect long time series of data (Flagg and Smith 1989; Emery and Thomson 1997). Time series analysis involves the study of sequential data, and this form of analysis has a wide variety of oceanographic applications (Emery and Thomson 1997).

Upon receiving raw binary ADCP data files from SAIC, a RD Instruments software program called BBLIST was used to convert echo intensity data from binary to ASCII format. Data were grouped into 30 minute ensembles, and each ensemble contained information on the date and time, as well as echo intensity data in 4m intervals for each of the four transducer beams. The acoustic backscatter data from each of the four beams were averaged to obtain a single representative value of backscatter intensity for the water column at each depth bin.

To better define the association among variables affecting the echo intensity, a modified version of the sonar equation was applied to raw ADCP data (Deines 1999). The equation was used to solve for the backscatter coefficient, S_v. The equation follows:

$$S_v = C + 10\log_{10}((T_x + 273.16)R^2) - L_{DBM} - P_{DBW} + 2\alpha R + K_c(E-E_r)$$

where S_v = backscattering strength (dB), T_x = temperature of transducer (°C), R = range along the beam to the scatterers (m), L_{DBM} = $10\log_{10}$ transmit pulse length (m), P_{DBW} = $10\log_{10}$ transmit power (Watts), α = absorption coefficient of water (dB/m), K_c = factory calibration factor provided by RDI, E = echo intensity, and E_r = real-time reference level of echo intensity.

An important part of oceanographic data processing involves the application of digital filters to smooth time series and remove frequency fluctuations from given frequency bands. Low-pass filters eliminate high-frequency fluctuations while allowing low-frequency signals to pass through (Emery and Thomson 1997). A 40-hour low-pass filter was applied to the DeSoto Canyon backscatter intensity data to remove fluctuations in tidal and local inertial frequencies and to allow analysis of weekly to monthly temporal variability in acoustic backscatter intensity. Both unfiltered and low-pass filtered versions of the acoustic data were used in this study.

After S_v calculations were made and a low-pass filter was applied to the data, linear interpolation was used to fill short gaps in the time series between deployment periods. These hourly to day-long gaps occurred approximately every four months and resulted from the retrieval of instruments from the water followed by servicing and redeployment. This gap-filling process provided continuous 25-month time series of acoustic backscatter intensity. Procedures to estimate S_v, fill gaps, and filter the data were written using the visual data analysis software program PV-Wave.

For each of the twelve moored ADCPs, six representative depth bins were selected for data analysis. These depths were selected to determine mean acoustic backscatter patterns in near-surface, middle, and near-instrument waters. For instruments suspended at 80 meters in the water column, data analyses were made at 14 and 26m, 38 and 50m, and 62 and 70m. Data analyses were made at 20 and 32m, 44 and 56m, and 72 and 80m for instruments suspended at 90 meters depth. Selection of depth bins for analysis was based on two important factors. Data from the surface depth bins were not selected for data analysis due to side lobe contamination from surface reflections, and bottom bins nearest the ADCPs produced unreliable results related to residual transducer ringing.

Continuous two-year time series of acoustic backscatter data from eight moorings (A2, A3, B2, C1, C2, C3, D2, E1) were analyzed for this study. Technical problems with some of the data from moorings A1, B1, and D1 prevented the use of the full two years of ABI data, but selected portions of data were used from these sites. Specifically, mooring A1 was out of the water more than 24 hours during service and redeployment periods, so multi-day gaps occurred within the ABI record. These gaps were not filled, but backscatter data from individual deployment periods were used in conjunction with continuous time series from the remaining moorings. Mooring B1 was lost sometime after November 1997, and it could not be located during the instrument servicing and redeployment period in April 1998. Thus, only data from the first three deployment periods at mooring B1 (March 1997 - November 1997) were used for time series analysis. Mooring D1 was moored at 99m below the surface during deployment one, but was re-deployed at 80m for each of the remaining five deployments. Thus, data from deployment one at D1 was not included in the two-year time series analysis due to the depth discrepancy.

Acoustic backscatter data from mooring B3 were not included at all in this study. The ABI record for this mooring showed large amplitude jump shifts in acoustic backscatter intensity in all depth bins, so these data were considered to be unreliable. The cause of these jump shifts is unknown.

7

2.2 Biological Data Collection

2.2.1 NEGOM Project Description

Sponsored by the U.S. Minerals Management Service (MMS), the Northeastern Gulf of Mexico (NEGOM) Physical Oceanography Program: Chemical Oceanography and Hydrography Study included measurements to characterize the spatial distributions of chemical, physical, and biological variables over the shelf and upper slope of the northeastern Gulf of Mexico (NEGOM; OCS Contract 1435-01-97-CT-30851). This study encompassed a total of nine seasonally distributed oceanographic research cruises in the region extending from the Mississippi River delta to Tampa, Florida between the coast and the 1000 meter isobath. Cruises were conducted over a three year period, a portion of which corresponded to the deployment time of the 12 EIS ADCPs. Cruise dates were as follows: Cruise N1: November 16-26, 1997, Cruise N2 : May 4-15, 1998, Cruise N3: July 25-August 9, 1998, Cruise N4: November 12-25, 1998, Cruise N5: May 15-28, 1999, Cruise N6: August 15-28, 1999, Cruise N7: November 12-23, 1999, Cruise N8: April 14-26, 2000, and Cruise N9: July 28-August 8, 2000. On each of the nine cruises approximately 96 hydrographic stations were occupied for measurements and sample collection. Data collection included continuous vertical profiles of temperature and conductivity versus depth (CTD) and light transmission/ penetration in addition to bottle samples for dissolved oxygen, nutrients, phytoplankton pigments, suspended particulate matter, particulate organic carbon, and salinity. Samples were collected from the surface to near bottom at each hydrographic station. Figure 2.2.1-1 depicts the cruise track of NEGOM cruise three and the locations of the moored ADCPs are labeled.

2.2.2 Zooplankton Collection

To help interpret the ABI data, zooplankton collections were made on four cruises to the NE Gulf of Mexico between May 1998 and May 1999. These collections were made during the second (N2), third (N3), fourth (N4), and fifth (N5) NEGOM hydrographic survey cruises (see section 2.2.1 for details). All collections were made at the closest approach to each of the moored ADCPs. Collections were made less than two miles (3 km) from each of the moorings A1, A2, C2, and E1, and tows were made within eight miles (13 km) or less from moorings B2, C1, and D1. A total of 43 zooplankton samples were collected during the four cruises, with 11 net tows made during N2, 15 tows made during N3, 12 tows made during N4, and 5 tows made during cruise N5.

All zooplankton collections were made with a one-meter diameter net of mesh size 333 μm. At the nearest approach to each of the moored ADCPs, the net was towed obliquely from the surface to 100-m depth and back to the surface. The volume of water filtered was measured with a General Oceanics flow meter strung across the mouth of the net. Upon retrieving the net on deck, the net was rinsed and zooplankton assemblages

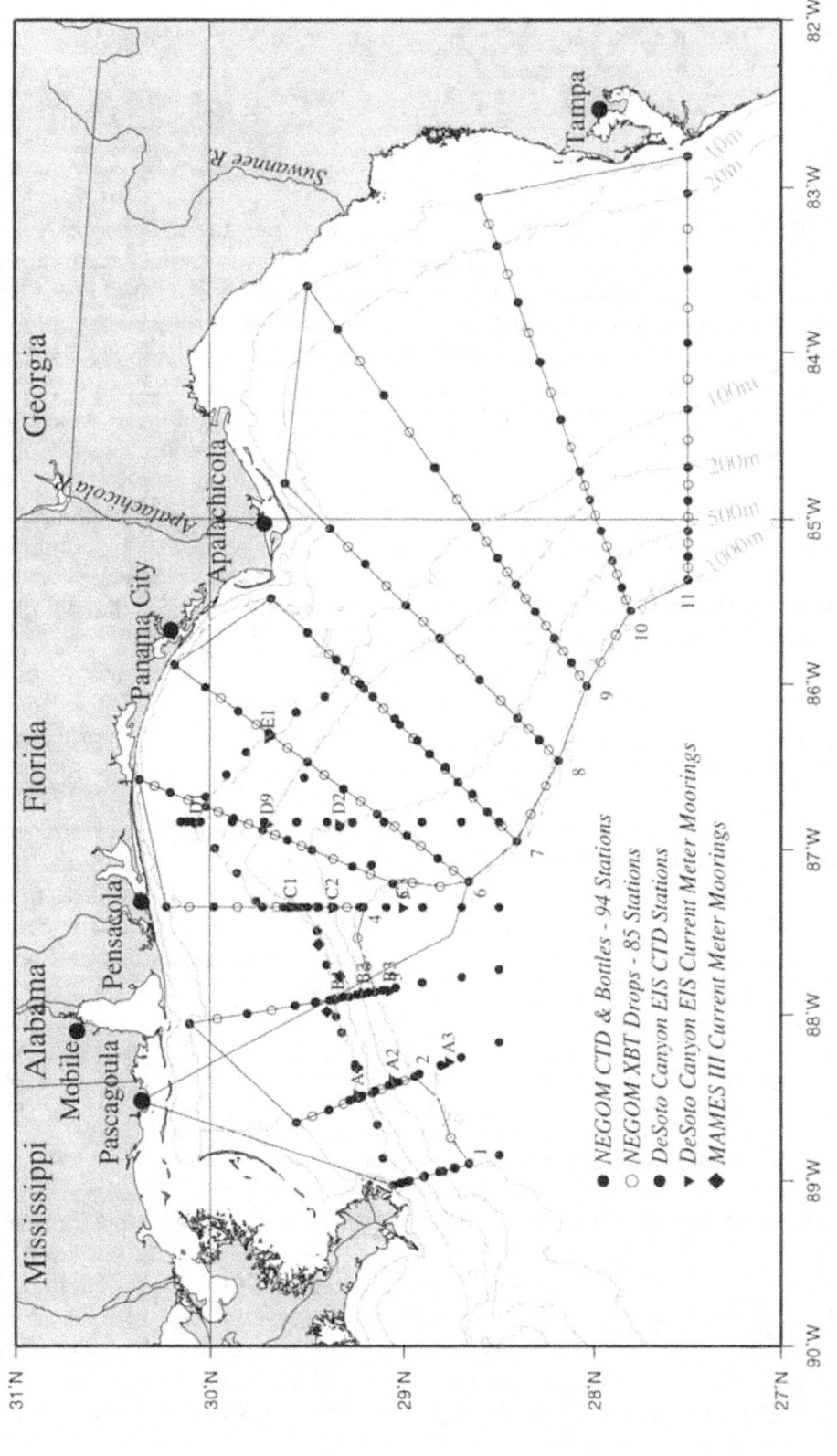

Fig. 2.2.1-1. Cruise track of NEGOM 3. Locations of DeSoto Canyon ADCPs are labeled.

9

were collected from the cod end. Samples were placed in plastic jars and preserved with buffered formalin for further analysis.

2.2.3 Analysis of Zooplankton Samples

Wet displacement biomass serves as a summary measure of zooplankton standing stock integrated for the upper 100 m of the water column , so wet displacement volumes were measured for all zooplankton samples collected during NEGOM cruises. Samples were size-fractionated through a 2-mm mesh screen, and wet displacement volume was again measured on the fraction of zooplankton < 2 mm. Organisms in the size range of 2 mm and greater are considered to be significant scatterers of acoustic energy. This size distinction is based on the speed of sound in water (1500 m/s) and the wavelength of the emitted acoustic signal (~ 5 mm for 300 kHz instruments). Acoustic waves can generally detect objects one quarter of the wavelength (Emery and Thomson 1997). All organisms in the > 2 mm size fraction were enumerated and grouped into broad taxonomic categories. The categories of organisms > 2mm included larval fish, squid paralarvae, juvenile and adult euphausiids, juvenile and adult decapods, other crustaceans, chaetognaths, siphonophores, meroplanktonic anthozoan larvae, salps and doliolids, medusae and ctenophores, pteropods and hard-shelled plankton, and all other macroplankton. Because the quantity and intensity of acoustic backscatter recorded depends in part upon the size of sound scatterers, the length frequency of decapods and other crustaceans was measured and organisms were placed in size categories ranging from < 3 mm to > 3 cm.

Net tow data collected during four NEGOM cruises were analyzed to identify seasonal signals in total biomass as well as seasonal signals in specific groups of organisms. To further investigate the diel variability of zooplankton biomass, net tow data were separated by time of tow into daylight and night time zooplankton collections. The average plankton collected per tow was calculated for both the day time and night time.

3.0 Results

3.1 Comparison of Physical and Biological Data

3.1.1 Relationship Between Acoustic Backscatter and Zooplankton Biomass

Zooplankton collections made during the three NEGOM cruises conducted while the ADCP moorings were in the DeSoto Canyon area served as sea truth for acoustic backscatter data. Values for zooplankton biomass collected during those three cruises were compared to acoustic backscatter intensity data recorded during the same time period. Zooplankton data collected during cruise N5 (May 1999) were not included in this analysis, as the ADCPs were removed from the water in April 1999 and there were no corresponding acoustic data for this cruise. Highest total zooplankton biomass was collected during cruise N2 conducted during May of 1998. Average plankton per tow collected during that cruise was 0.24 ml/m^3. Lowest biomass was collected during cruise N4 (November 1998), and the average plankton collected per tow during that cruise was 0.1 ml/m^3. Average plankton values collected were clearly highest during night time hours on cruises N2 and N4. Zooplankton biomass values ranged from a low value of 0.09 ml/m^3 collected during daylight hours to 0.27 ml/m^3 collected during dark hours. High night time values of zooplankton biomass are a consequence of the diel vertical migration of zooplankters into the upper water column during hours of darkness. Table 3.1.1-1 summarizes zooplankton biomass values collected during four NEGOM cruises.

Table 3.1.1-1. Summary of zooplankton collections made during NEGOM cruises.

CRUISE	DATES	# OF TOWS	AVERAGE PLANKTON PER TOW (ml/m^3)	AVERAGE PLANKTON PER TOW: DAY TIME (ml/m^3)	AVERAGE PLANKTON PER TOW: NIGHT TIME (ml/m^3)
NEGOM 2	May 4-15 1998	11	0.24	0.19	0.27
NEGOM 3	July 25-August 9 1998	15	0.15	0.16	0.13
NEGOM 4	November 12-25 1998	12	0.10	0.09	0.12
NEGOM 5	May 15-28 1999	5	0.18	0.12	0.23

To compare acoustic data with total biomass collected throughout the region on three NEGOM cruises, acoustic data from each mooring were compiled to produce a single average backscatter intensity value for the NEGOM region during each of the cruises N2, N3, and N4. Highest acoustic backscatter was recorded in May 1998 (cruise N2), with lowest acoustic backscatter recorded during November 1998. Figure 3.1.1-1 displays total plankton biomass collected during three NEGOM cruises with accompanying acoustic backscatter intensity values for the corresponding time periods.

Although zooplankton collections were made throughout the NEGOM region on each of three cruises which overlapped with ADCP measurements, not all collections directly corresponded to ADCP mooring locations. To better define the relationship between backscatter and biomass, values for the two variables were compared only for those ADCP moorings with zooplankton collections made within a 20-kilometer (12-mile) radius. To obtain backscatter data corresponding to each of the zooplankton tows, a single average water column backscatter value was calculated from the six representative

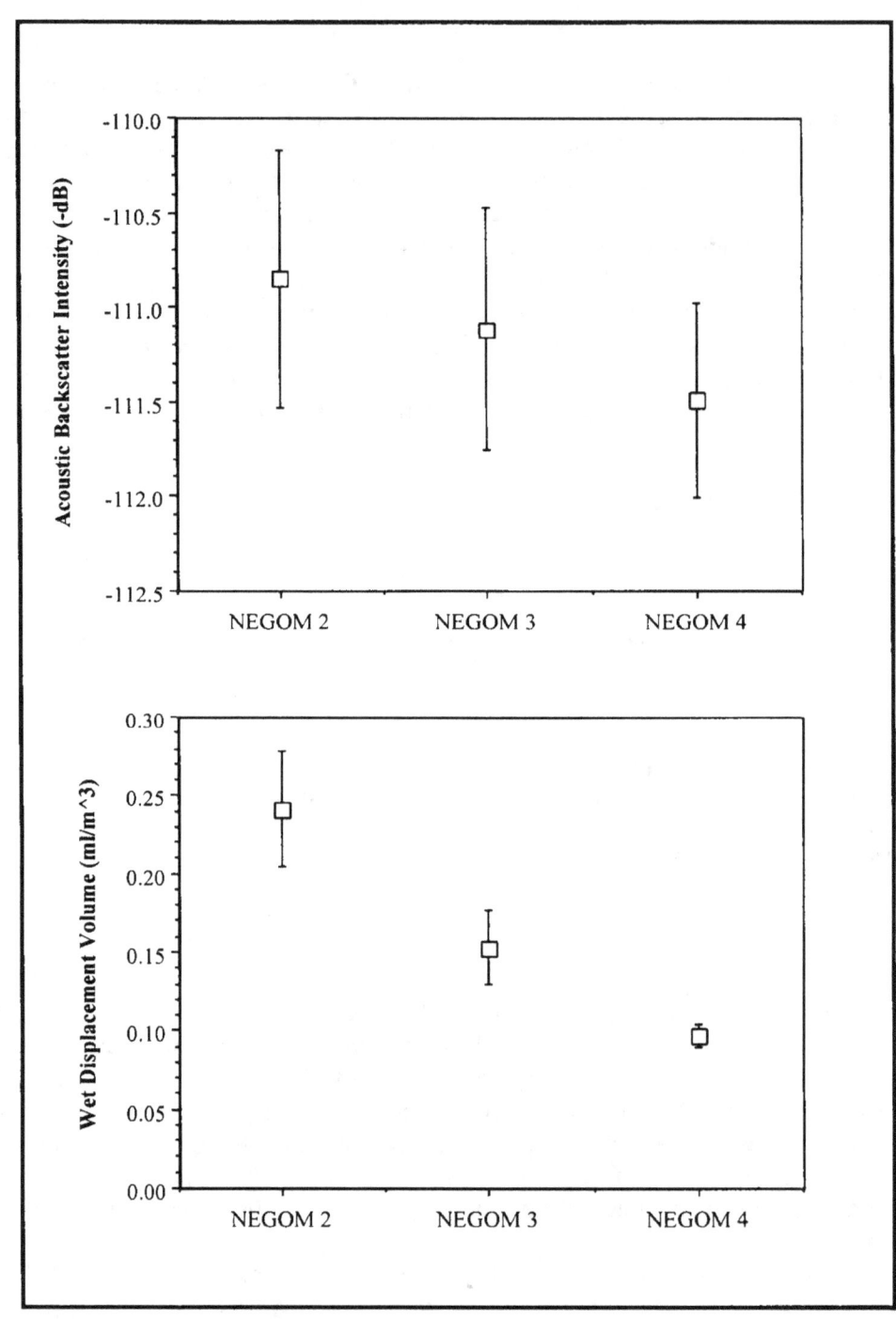

Figure 3.3.1-1. Comparison between average acoustic backscatter intensity (upper) and average zooplankton wet displacement volume collected in net tows (lower). Boxes show the mean and whiskers show the standard error of the mean.

depth bins at each location of interest. Unfiltered acoustic backscatter data were averaged over a two- hour time block centered around each of the zooplankton tows (one hour prior to tow and one hour after tow). A regression analysis was performed using a total of 21 backscatter/zooplankton data pairs.

Figure 3.1.1-2 displays the results of the regression analysis between acoustic backscatter intensity and directly corresponding zooplankton tows made on three NEGOM cruises (n = 21). Curved lines indicate the 95% confidence interval for the mean response, and approximately 60% of the data points fell within these intervals. To see if there was a positive linear relationship between acoustic backscatter intensity and zooplankton biomass, a statistical t-test was conducted to evaluate the slope of the regression trend line. Results of this test showed the slope of the line to be greater than zero, indicating a positive relationship between the two variables at the 0.025 significance level.

The relationship between backscatter and biomass was again plotted using only biomass data for organisms 2 mm and greater. Figure 3.1.1-3 shows the results of this regression analysis (n = 21). Again the 95% confidence intervals for the mean response are marked by curved lines. A statistical t-test proved the slope of the regression trend line to be significantly greater than zero. Results were significant at the 0.01 significance level, indicating a stronger relationship between acoustic backscatter and organisms > 2 mm than that of acoustic backscatter and total zooplankton biomass.

3.1.2 Correlation Analysis

Appendix A shows 25-month running plots of ABI data for six representative depths at the 11 sites with useable data. At each site, ABI generally averaged 3-4 dB lower near the surface (z = 14-32m) than deeper in the water column. This general increase in ABI with increasing depth in the upper 100m has been reported previously from analyses of ABI data collected by ship-mounted narrowband ADCPs (Zimmerman and Biggs 1999; Ressler 2001). In those surveys, highest ABI usually occurred between the base of the wind mixed layer and the depth of the 19°C isotherm. Within this zone a deep chlorophyll maximum (DCM) was often found at the interface between the nitracline (10 μM/L nitrate at 19°C) and adequate irradiance to allow net photosynthesis to proceed. The locally elevated ABI there is believed to be a consequence of the locally high concentrations of herbivorous zooplankton present to graze the primary production of the DCM.

To determine the effect of depth and mooring separation distance on acoustic backscatter intensity and to define vertical and horizontal scales associated with these backscatter data, a systematic correlation analysis was carried out using backscatter time series data. For each of the mooring locations, correlation coefficients were calculated among the six representative depth bins selected for study. Adjacent 4-meter depth bins

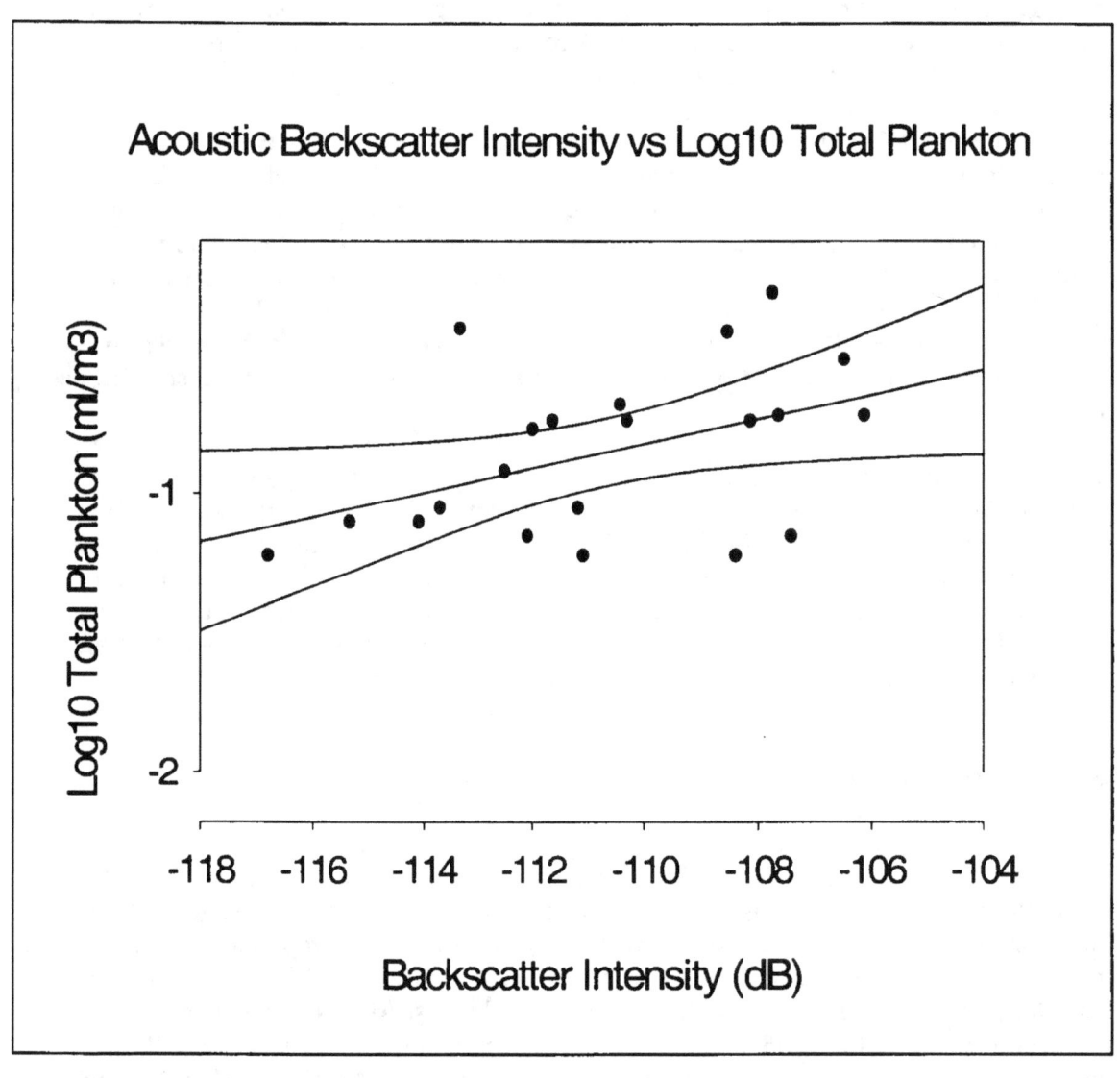

Figure 3.1.1-2. Regression analysis between acoustic backscatter intensity and total plankton collected during NEGOM cruises.

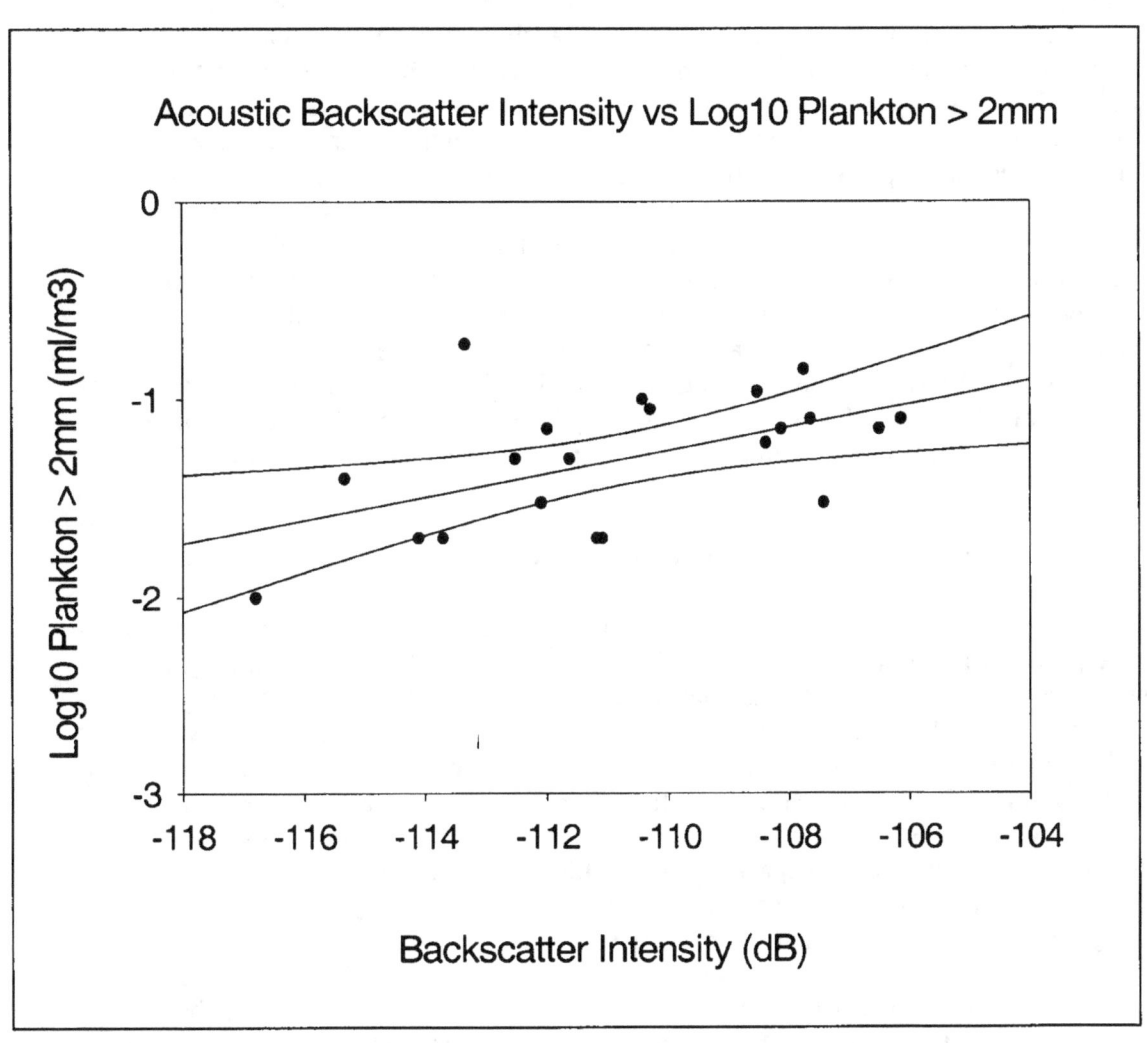

Figure 3.1.1-3. Regression analysis between acoustic backscatter intensity and plankton > 2mm.

were significantly correlated, but correlation values decreased as the vertical distance between depth bins increased. As a consequence, there was no significant correlation among the six representative depth bins selected at each ADCP mooring location, as each of these bins was separated by a vertical distance of approximately 12m. Table 3.1.2-1 shows an example of correlation coefficients calculated among depth bins at each of six mooring locations representative of the study area (A1, A2, A3, C1, C2, and C3).

Cross correlation of one common upper water depth bin at all eleven moorings was carried out to better define the horizontal scales of acoustic backscatter data. However, none of the cross correlation values were statistically significant. Of the twelve moored ADCPs, those located nearest one another were separated by a distance of nine miles (16 km). This indicates that horizontal scales of acoustic backscatter intensity are generally less than 20 km between mooring locations. Table 3.1.2-2 highlights correlation coefficients calculated for one common bin at eleven mooring locations.

3.1.3 Spectral Analysis of Acoustic Time Series

Spectral analysis is performed on time series data to examine the variance of the time series as a function of frequency. The frequency distributions of oceanographic spectra are often described by the colors red, blue, and white of the electromagnetic spectrum. A "red" spectrum shows a decrease in spectral density as frequency increases. This is analogous to the color red on the visible spectrum, as red corresponds to longer wavelengths and lower frequencies. If the magnitude of a spectrum increases as frequency increases, the spectrum is described as "blue". A "white" spectrum shows roughly equal amplitudes in spectral density throughout the range in frequency. Oceanic long-term variability, referring to periods longer than several days, commonly has a red variance spectrum (Emery and Thomson 1997).

Spectral analysis was performed on the 24-month unfiltered acoustic backscatter data for each of the moored ADCPs. The resulting spectra were plotted to show energy spectral density (energy per unit time; y-axis) as a function of frequency (cycles per day; x-axis). All spectra were red, exhibiting a marked decrease in spectral density with increasing frequency. Figure 3.1.3-1 includes examples of such spectra. The spectral density indicates there was significant weekly to monthly variability in the acoustic time series records.

Evident in all spectra of unfiltered acoustic data was a sharp peak in energy density centered at one cycle per day. The peaks, seen in all depth bins at each mooring, reached maximum energy density values of approximately 0.1 dB^{-2} s^{-2} hr^{-1}. This increase in energy density centered at one cycle per day is indicative of the diel vertical migration of zooplankton in the water column. The word 'diel' describes events that occur with 24-hour periodicity, and the diel vertical migration of zooplankton is characterized by upward migration towards the surface at night followed by a return to deeper water in the

16

Table 3.1.2-1. Correlation coefficients (r values) calculated between vertical depth bins at six DeSoto Canyon ADCP mooring locations. Correlations were calculated using unfiltered acoustic backscatter intensity data.

A1	14m	26m	38m	50m	62m	70m
14m	1.0	0.68	0.49	0.35	0.24	0.17
26m	-	1.0	0.73	0.55	0.38	0.28
38m	-	-	1.0	0.76	0.52	0.40
50m	-	-	-	1.0	0.71	0.54
62m	-	-	-	-	1.0	0.78
70m	-	-	-	-	-	1.0

A2	24m	32m	44m	56m	72m	80m
24m	1.0	0.770	0.506	0.331	0.113	0.056
32m	-	1.0	0.737	0.522	0.236	0.197
44m	-	-	1.0	0.741	0.363	0.318
56m	-	-	-	1.0	0.593	0.513
72m	-	-	-	-	1.0	0.817
80m	-	-	-	-	-	1.0

A3	14m	26m	38m	50m	62m	70m
14m	1.0	0.767	0.643	0.515	0.282	0.217
26m	-	1.0	0.837	0.659	0.329	0.311
38m	-	-	1.0	0.813	0.435	0.400
50m	-	-	-	1.0	0.572	0.489
62m	-	-	-	-	1.0	0.676
70m	-	-	-	-	-	1.0

C1	14m	26m	38m	50m	62m	70m
14m	1.0	0.651	0.380	0.270	0.158	0.147
26m	-	1.0	0.693	0.495	0.316	0.239
38m	-	-	1.0	0.755	0.500	0.387
50m	-	-	-	1.0	0.690	0.551
62m	-	-	-	-	1.0	0.751
70m	-	-	-	-	-	1.0

C2	20m	32m	44m	56m	72m	80m
20m	1.0	0.634	0.354	0.225	0.175	0.172
32m	-	1.0	0.715	0.525	0.382	0.326
44m	-	-	1.0	0.751	0.512	0.420
56m	-	-	-	1.0	0.698	0.571
72m	-	-	-	-	1.0	0.858
80m	-	-	-	-	-	1.0

C3	14m	26m	38m	50m	62m	70m
14m	1.0	0.676	0.526	0.441	0.285	0.231
26m	-	1.0	0.840	0.707	0.501	0.479
38m	-	-	1.0	0.828	0.584	0.556
50m	-	-	-	1.0	0.730	0.669
62m	-	-	-	-	1.0	0.840
70m	-	-	-	-	-	1.0

Table 3.1.2-2. Correlation coefficients (r values) calcuted between one upper-water depth bin at 11 ADCP mooring locations. Correlations were calculated using unfiltered acoustic backscatter intensity data.

	A1 26m	A2 24m	A3 26m	B1 26m	B2 20m	C1 26m	C2 20m	C3 26m	D1 26m	D2 20m	E1 26m
A1 26m	1.0	0.341	0.173	-0.046	0.168	0.281	0.019	0.104	0.200	0.020	0.089
A2 24m	-	1.0	0.326	0.273	0.414	0.088	0.274	0.424	0.318	0.330	0.065
A3 26m	-	-	1.0	-0.058	-0.005	-0.056	-0.151	-0.127	0.251	-0.074	0.004
B1 26m	-	-	-	1.0	0.278	0.292	0.358	0.442	0.208	0.304	0.233
B2 20m	-	-	-	-	1.0	0.128	0.421	0.304	0.402	0.437	0.139
C1 26m	-	-	-	-	-	1.0	0.200	0.364	0.165	0.203	0.315
C2 20m	-	-	-	-	-	-	1.0	0.320	0.424	0.577	0.222
C3 26m	-	-	-	-	-	-	-	1.0	0.317	0.356	0.146
D1 26m	-	-	-	-	-	-	-	-	1.0	0.499	0.379
D2 20m	-	-	-	-	-	-	-	-	-	1.0	0.237
E1 26m	-	-	-	-	-	-	-	-	-	-	1.0

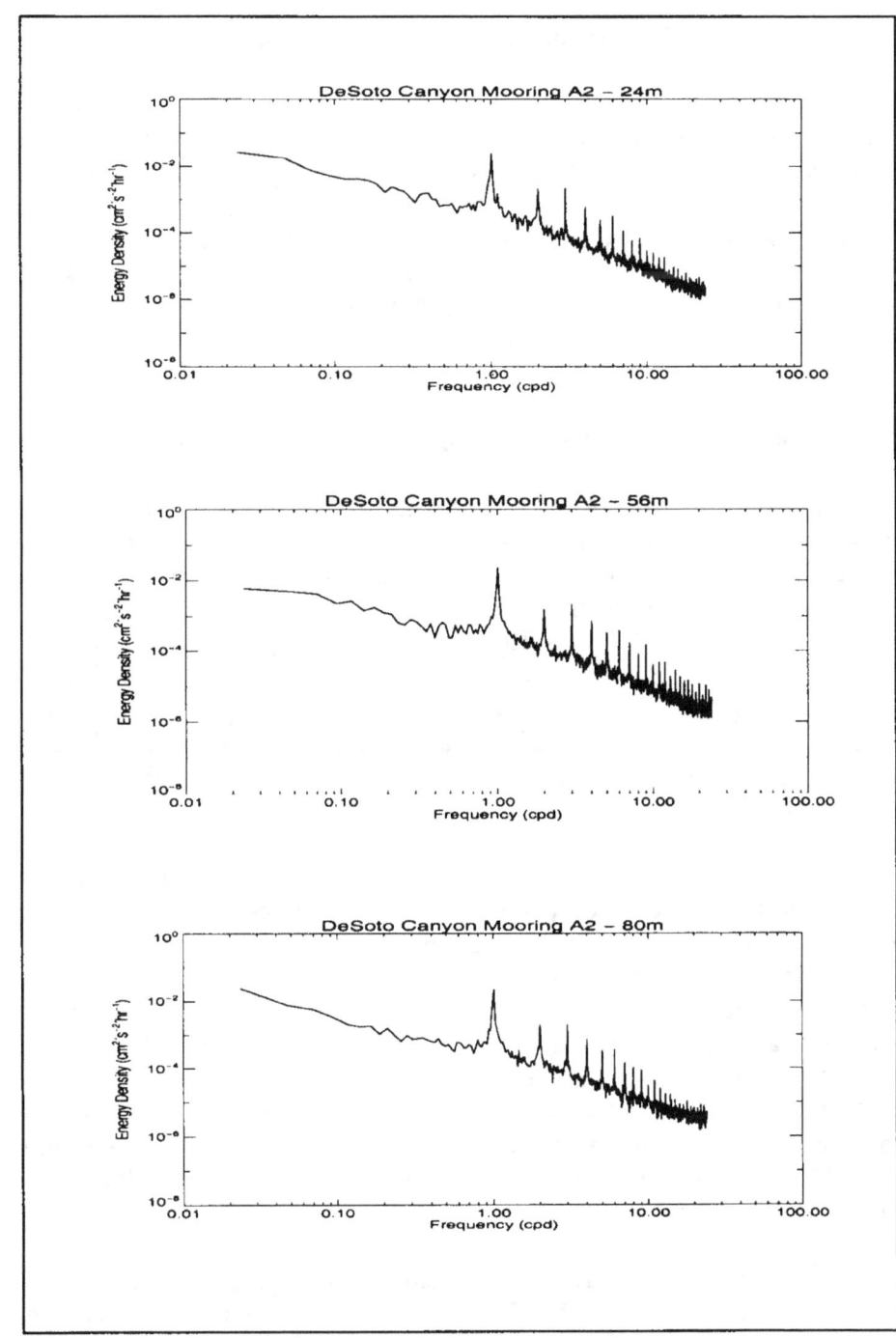

Figure 3.1.3-1. Variance spectra of unfiltered acoustic backscatter data. Spectra were generated using upper-, mid-, and deep-water backscatter data from mooring A2. The large peak centered at one cycle per day is a consequence of the diel vertical migration of zooplankton in the water column.

daytime. Smaller recurring high-frequency peaks seen in all spectra are harmonics of the fundamental frequency.

To better analyze the low frequency variability of acoustic backscatter intensity, spectral analysis was also performed on the 40-hour low-pass filtered acoustic data. All depth bins at each mooring showed marked variance in energy density on the 3-4 day (0.25-0.33 cpd) to weekly-biweekly (0.07-0.14 cpd) time scale. Figure 3.1.3-2 compares a spectrum of unfiltered ABI data with a spectrum of 40-hour low-pass filtered ABI data. Spectra for near-surface, middle, and near-instrument ABI data are shown in Appendix B.

3.1.4 Effect of Circulation Dynamics on Acoustic Backscatter Time Series

Spectral analysis of acoustic backscatter data showed there was low frequency variability (weekly to monthly) in backscatter intensity, so current velocity data recorded by the moored array of ADCPs were used to investigate the relationship between such low frequency acoustic variability and current flow in the DeSoto Canyon area. Working with the current velocity data, two-year time series of velocity components were generated at the closest possible depths to those selected for backscatter analysis. This consisted of generating paired current velocity time series for each depth of interest at the ADCP moorings. One time series contained data from the u component of the current vector (east-west), while the second time series consisted of data from the v component of the current vector (north-south).

To more accurately study the patterns of current flow in the northeastern Gulf of Mexico, u and v current velocity components were rotated to better match the bathymetry of the DeSoto Canyon area. Current components were rotated so that the v component was parallel to the prevailing isobath trends. Results of these rotations included time series of cross-slope (rotated u) and along-shelf (rotated v) current velocity components. Positive velocity values of the along-shelf component were indicative of flow from west to east, while negative values represented flow from east to west. Positive velocity values of the cross-slope component represented off-shore flow from shallow to deeper waters, and negative velocity values signified on-shore current flow from deep to shallow waters. Figure 3.1.4-1 includes representative time series of both cross-slope and along-shelf current velocity components.

Combined acoustic backscatter and rotated current data from six representative ADCP moorings (A1, A2, A3 and C1, C2, C3) were used to determine correlations between acoustic backscatter intensity and current flow in the DeSoto Canyon area. Due to unfilled inter-deployment gaps in the current records, all correlations between backscatter and current flow were made on a deployment by deployment basis. Correlation coefficients (r) were determined between backscatter and paired current components from the uppermost depth bin at each of the six selected ADCP locations.

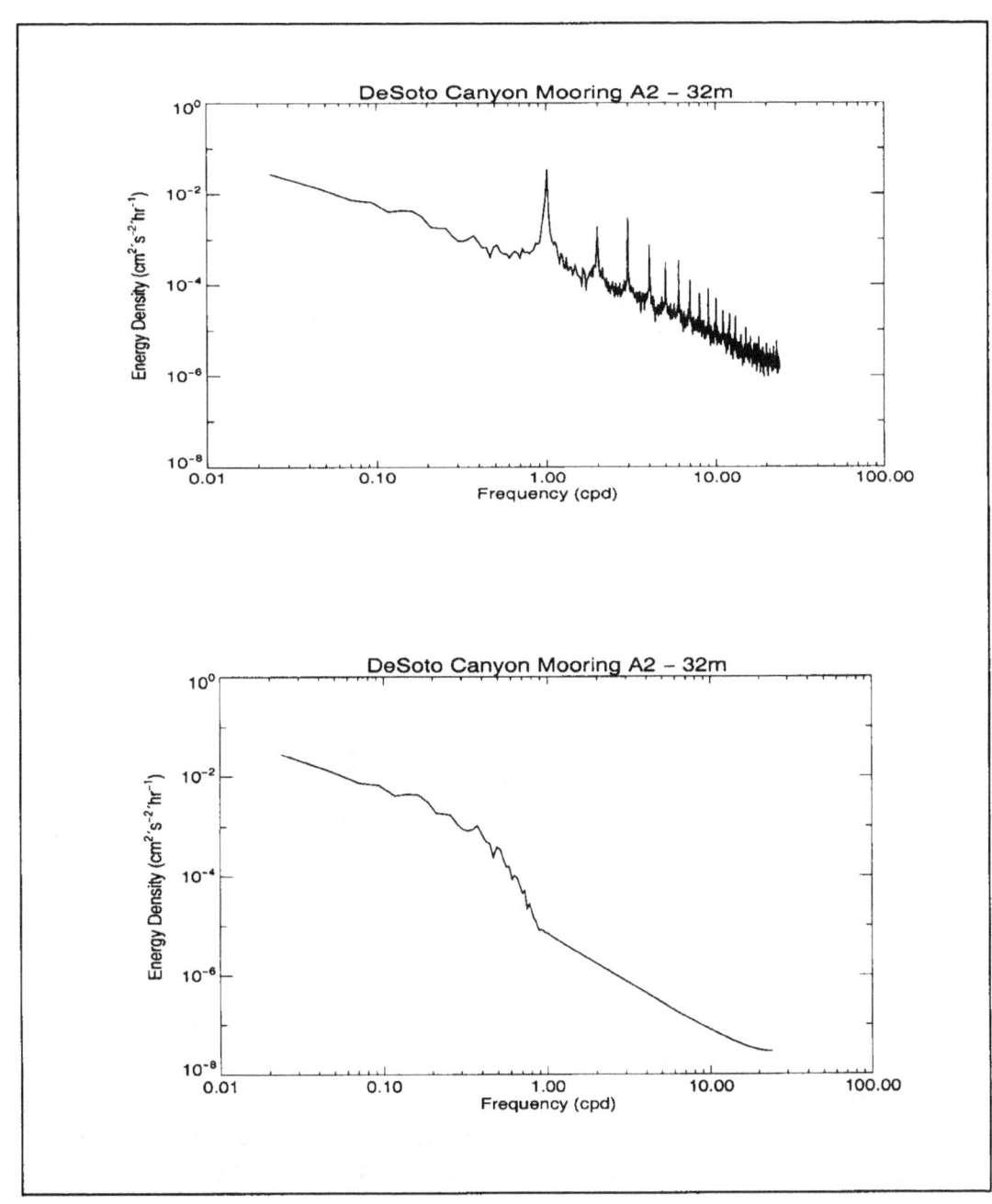

Figure 3.1.3-2. Variance spectra of unfiltered acoustic backscatter data (upper) and filtered acoustic backscatter data (lower). Spectral analysis of filtered acoustic data enables the study of low-frequency variability in backscatter intensity associated with current flow in the DeSoto Canyon area. Spectra were generated using data from the 32 m depth bin at mooring A2.

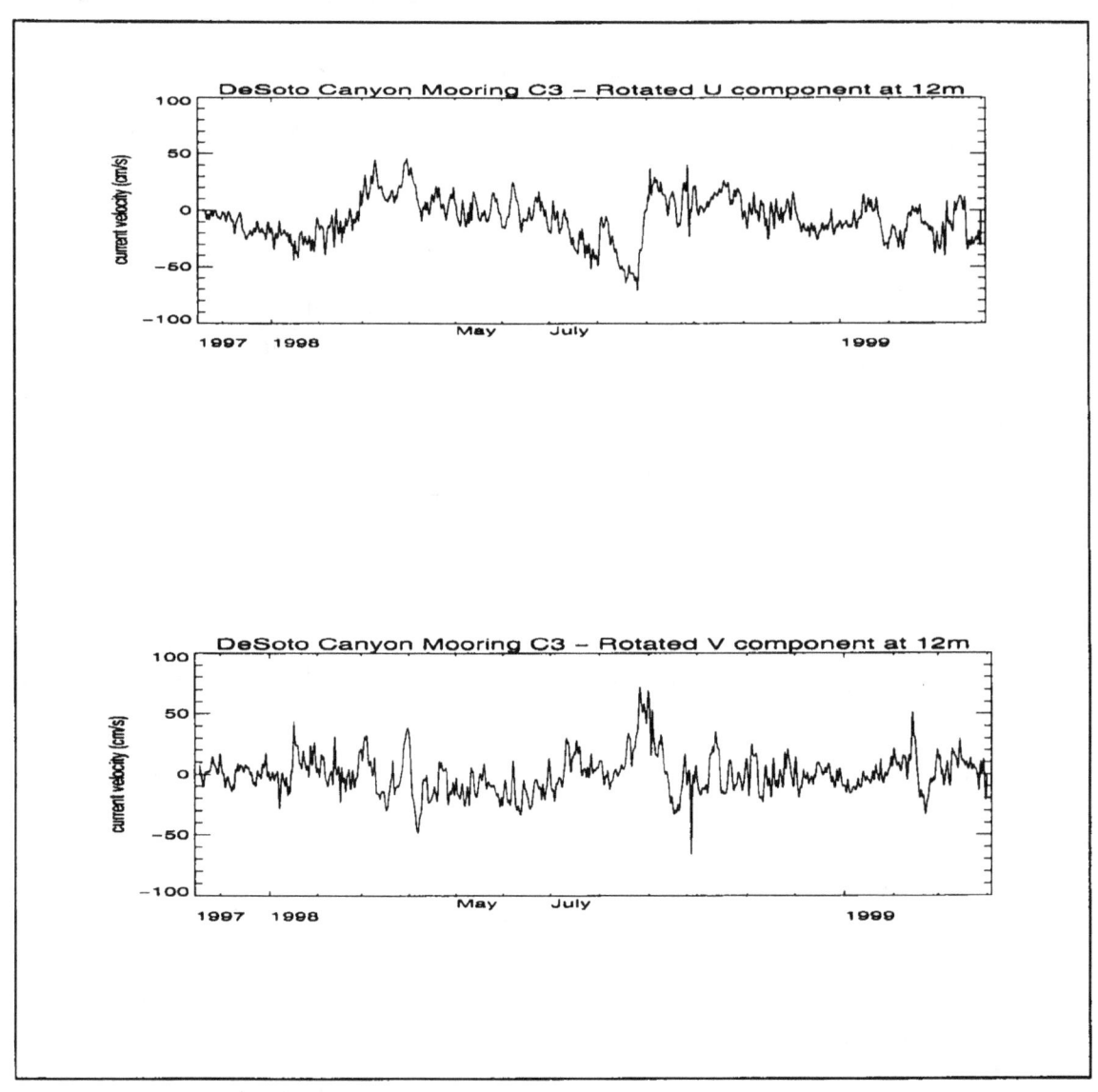

Figure 3.1.4-1. Examples of filtered cross-shelf (rotated *u*) and along-slope (rotated *v*) current velocity components at 12-m depth, mooring C3.

Such correlation analysis allowed us to distinguish patterns in the relationship between acoustic backscatter intensity and current flow in the northeastern Gulf. Of the six representative locations selected for combined backscatter and current analysis, four locations (A1, A2, A3, and C2) showed significant positive correlations between backscatter intensity and current velocity. These positive correlations occurred during deployment periods 2-5, July 1997 - December 1998.

Analysis of sea surface height anomaly (SSHA) plots for the corresponding time period revealed the presence of Loop Current Eddies (LCEs) and Warm Slope Eddies (WSEs) in the vicinity of the moored ADCPs. These eddies are regions of clockwise (anticyclonic) circulation. A small WSE was located off the southeastern coast of Louisiana in July of 1997, but this feature soon dissipated and was not evident in the monthly mean SSHA plot for August 1997. A larger WSE was evident in November of 1997, and at that time the feature was centered at the approximate location of 28.5° N, 88.0°W. This eddy persisted over the study region and was evident in SSHA plots through February of 1998 when it continued to move westward away from the mooring locations.

Another prominent feature seen in the monthly mean SSHA plots was LCE 'Gyre', which separated from the Loop Current in early summer 1998 and remained in the study area during the months of July - September 1998. The majority of the significant correlations calculated were between acoustic backscatter and cross-slope flow, but backscatter was also significantly correlated with along-shelf flow. Correlations between backscatter and the direction of current flow varied depending on the movement of mesoscale physical features described. Table 3.1.4-1 highlights all significant correlations between acoustic backscatter intensity and current flow in the DeSoto Canyon area.

3.2 Analysis of Storm Events

To look for an acoustic signature of intense wind mixing on acoustic backscatter, combined current velocity and backscatter data from the periods of Hurricane Georges and Hurricane Earl were studied in detail. Georges and Earl entered the Gulf of Mexico in late September and late August 1998 (respectively) and crossed the region of the moored DeSoto Canyon ADCPs. With maximum wind speeds near 175 mph, Hurricane Georges was the second strongest storm event within the Atlantic basin during 1998. Seven landfalls, ranging from the northeastern Caribbean to the Mississippi coast, occurred during Georges' 17 day track. The less intense Hurricane Earl produced winds as strong as 118 mph. Earl was responsible for significant storm surge flooding in the Big Bend area of Florida. Figure 3.2-1 shows storm tracks of hurricane events in the Gulf and their proximity to ADCP mooring locations.

Table 3.1.4-1. Statistically significant correlations (r values) between 40-hour low-pass filtered acoustic backscatter intensity data and 40-hour low-pass filtered rotated current velocity components.

Mooring	Deployment	Depth	Cross-Slope Correlations 1% significance	Cross-Slope Correlations 5% significance	Along-Shelf Correlations 1% significance	Along-Shelf Correlations 5% significance
A1	3	14m	0.085	*	*	*
A2	3	24m	0.146	*	*	*
A2	5	24m	0.316	*	*	*
A3	2	14m	0.434	*	0.178	*
A3	4	14m	*	0.259	*	*
A3	5	14m	0.332	*	*	*
C2	2	24m	*	*	0.534	*

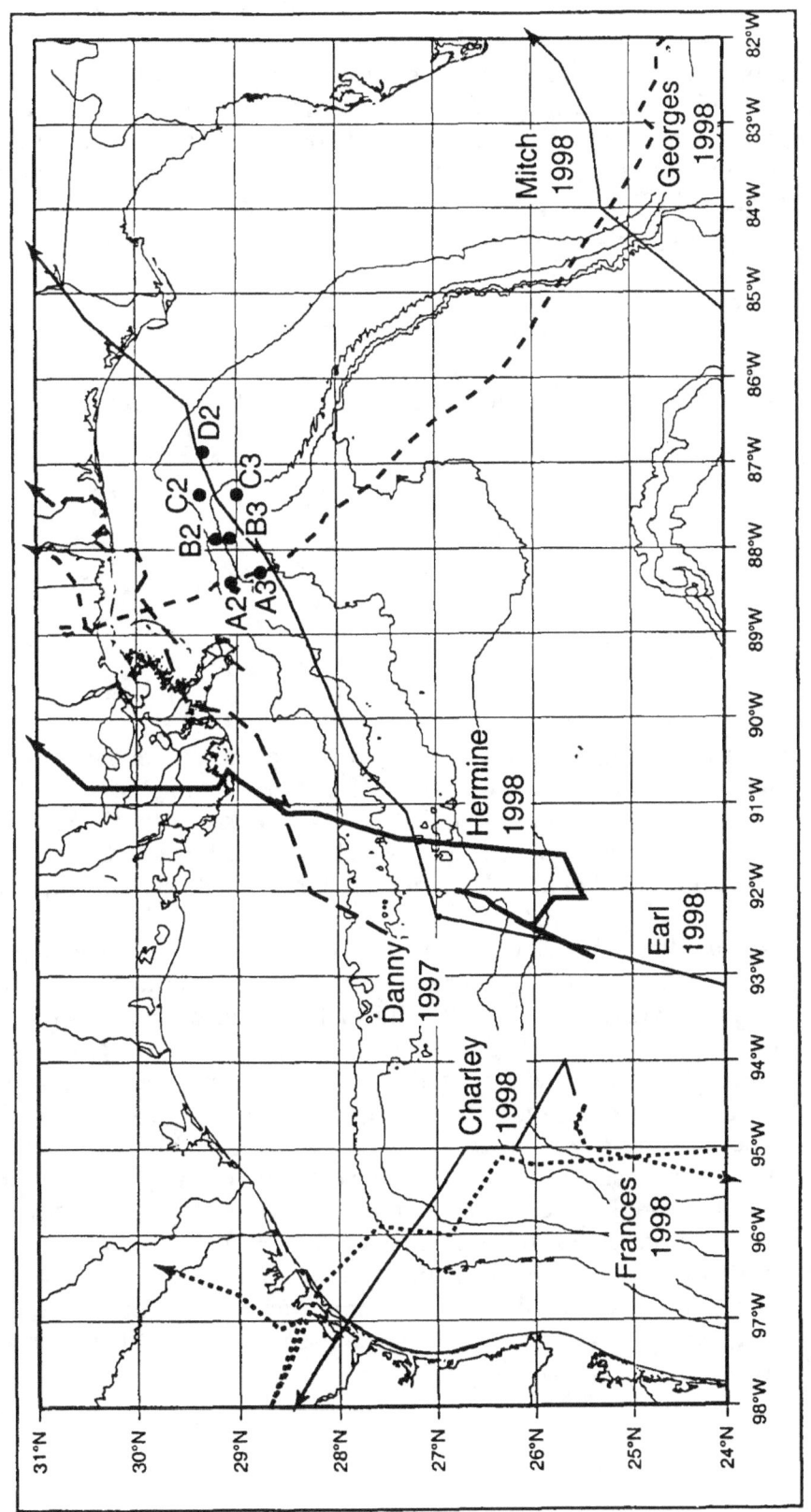

Figure 3.2-1. Tropical storm and hurricane tracks in the Gulf during the ADCP deployment period. Locations of ADCP moorings in water depths greater than 200 m are shown. This figure was used with permission and was originally included as part of the Deepwater Physical Oceanography Reanalysis and Synthesis of Historical Data: Synthesis Report (MMS Contract 1435-98-CT-30910).

3.2.1 Hurricane Georges

Tropical depression Georges originated as a tropical wave off Africa's west coast in early September, 1998. On September 16, the system was upgraded to a tropical storm while located approximately 700 miles (1126 km) west-southwest of the Cape Verde Islands. Continuing to move along a west-northwest course, the storm reached category-four status on September 19, 1998. Table 3.2.1-1 lists storm categories as defined by the Saffir-Simpson Scale of tropical storms.

Table 3.2.1-1. Saffir-Simpson scale of tropical storms.

CATEGORY	WINDS (MPH)	STORM SURGE (FT)
1	74-95	4-5
2	96-110	6-8
3	111-130	9-12
4	131-155	13-18
5	>155	>18

During its course, Hurricane Georges made several landfalls along the southeastern United States including Key West (FL) and Biloxi (MS). After making landfall at Biloxi on September 28, the system moved in a cyclonic loop over southern Mississippi for approximately six to twelve hours and then continued along a northeastern track. The storm dissipated on October 1, 1998 near the northeast Florida/southeast Georgia coast.

Time series of unfiltered acoustic backscatter data were compared to unfiltered current velocity data for the period of September 15-30, 1998. Data from moorings C3 (29.00°N, 87.35°W) and D2 (29.33°N, 86.85°W) showed a sudden dramatic increase in acoustic backscatter intensity accompanied by elevated north-south (v) and east-west (u) current velocity components. From September 27 - 28, north/south velocity components at mooring C3 changed from -20 cm/s to +100 cm/s in the upper and middle depth bins. This reversal in velocity values represents southerly flow at 20 cm/s followed by strong northerly flow at 100 cm/s. East/west velocity components changed from -80 cm/s to +90 cm/s, indicating westward flow at 80 cm/s turning to eastward flow at velocities of 90 cm/s. For the same period of September 27-28, mooring D2 showed an increase in northward flow from 10 cm/s to over 100 cm/s in the upper 20m of water. Flow alternated from 90 cm/s in the westward direction to approximately 70 cm/s in the eastward direction. Figures 3.2.1-1 and 3.2.1-2 compare acoustic backscatter intensity and current velocity components at moorings C3 and D2.

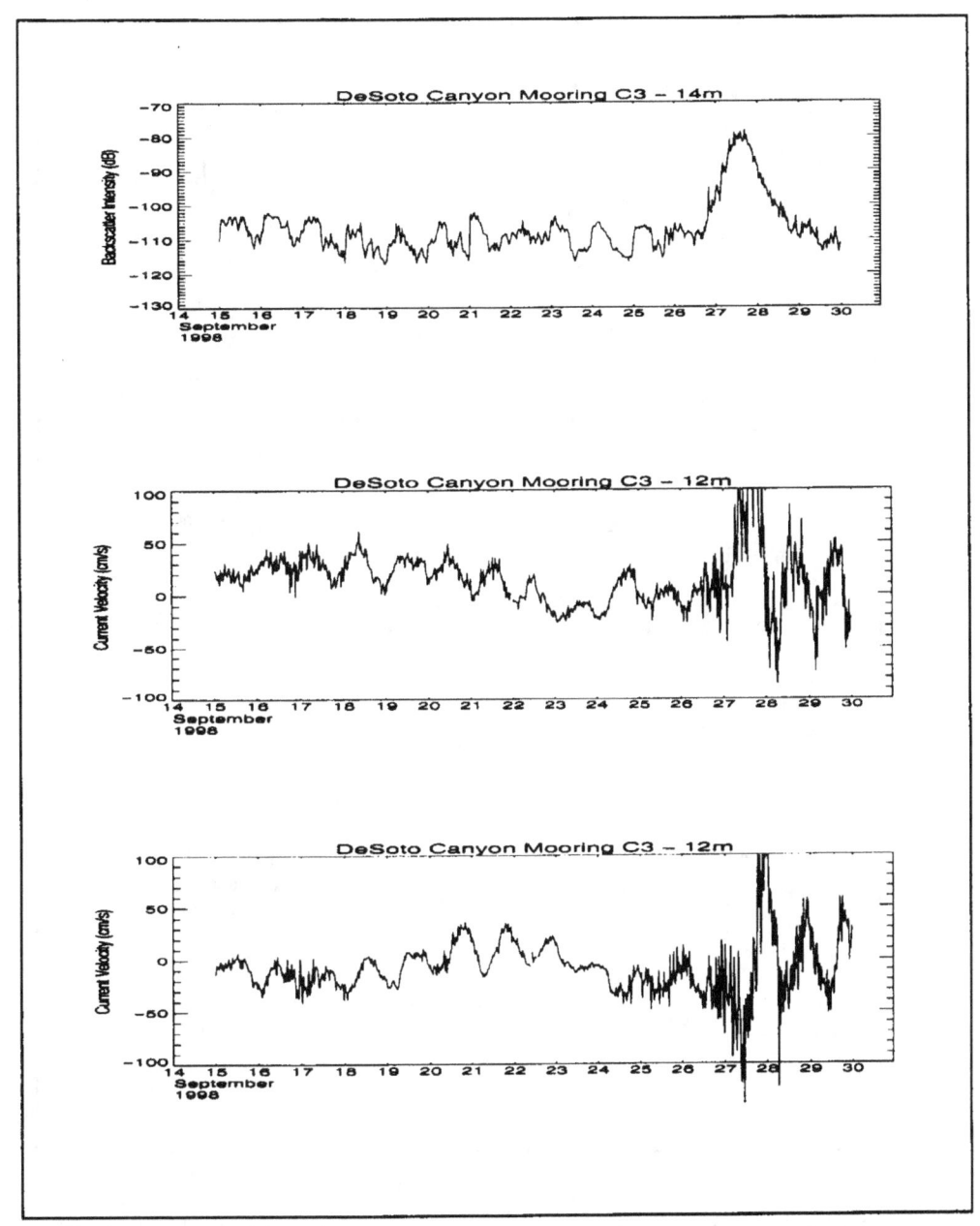

Figure 3.2.1-1. Comparisons between unfiltered acoustic backscatter intensity and unfiltered current velocity components during the period of Hurricane Georges. A time series of backscatter intensity is given in the upper figure. The middle figure depicts a time series of the N/S current velocity component, and the E/W current velocity component is depicted in the lower figure. Time series were generated using data from the uppermost depth bin at mooring C3.

27

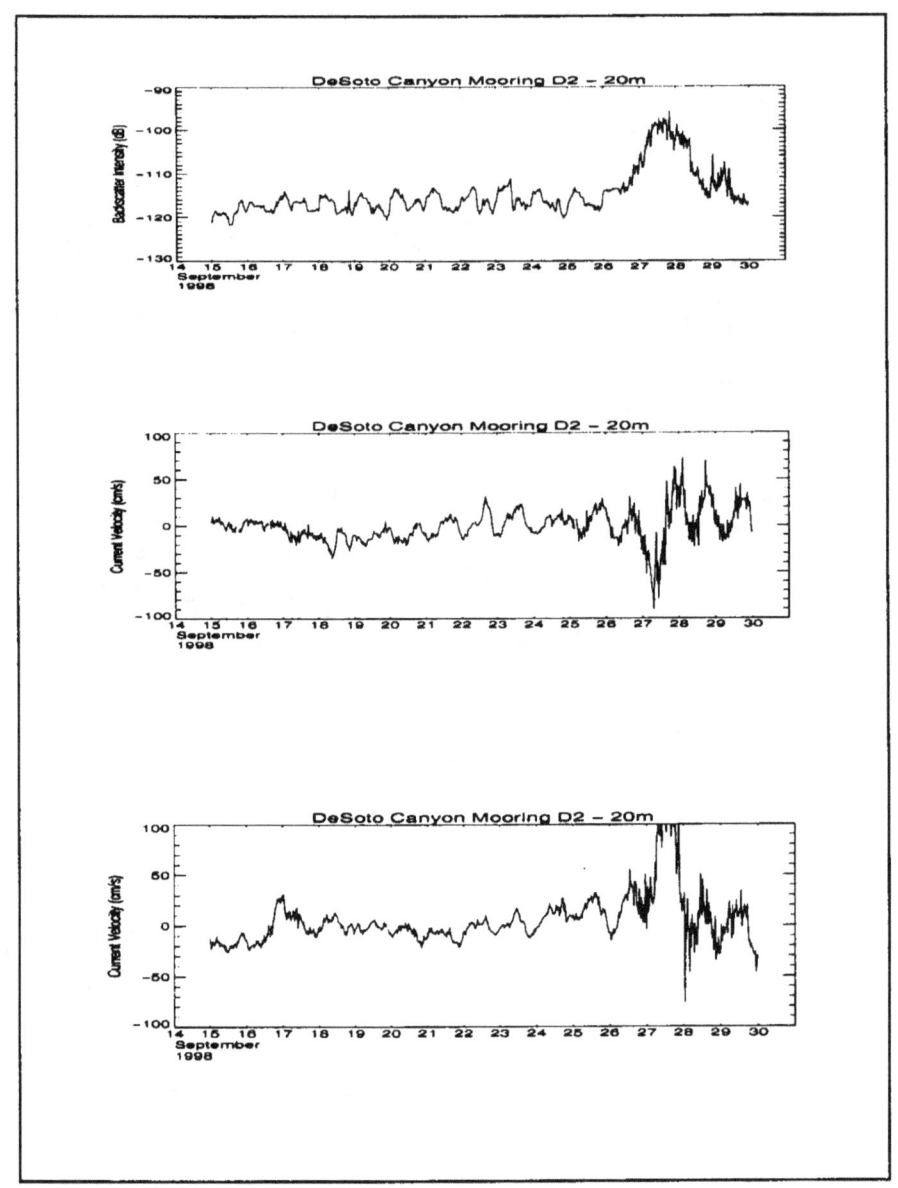

Figure 3.2.1-2. Comparisons between unfiltered acoustic backscatter intensity and unfiltered current velocity components during the period of Hurricane Georges. A time series of acoustic backscatter intensity is given in the upper figure. The middle figure depicts a time series of the E/W current velocity component, and the lower figure depicts a time series of the N/S current velocity component. Time series were generated using data from 20 m depth, mooring D2.

28

A single, broad peak in backscatter data was evident from September 27-30, 1998 in the 20-meter depth bin. This elevated backscatter response is only seen within the upper 20 m of water even though current velocity data showed enhanced velocity storm effects extending as deep as 44 m in the water column (see figures 3.2.1-1 and 3.2.1-2). Despite this broad peak in backscatter during the latter portion of the storm, the remainder of the unfiltered acoustic backscatter time series for the storm period showed regular diel alternation in backscatter intensity. The diel alternation is characterized by high levels of acoustic backscatter intensity at night followed by a rapid drop to lower daytime backscatter intensity values. This 24-hour cycle of backscatter intensity fluctuation is indicative of the diel vertical migration of zooplankton in the water column.

Using the u and v current velocity components, current speeds were calculated and times series of current speed were compared to acoustic backscatter intensity during the period of Hurricane Georges. Forty-hour low-pass filtered backscatter data were compared to filtered current speed data, and there was significant correlation between backscatter intensity and current speed in the upper 20 m. Figure 3.2.1-3 compares backscatter intensity with current speed at mooring D2.

3.2.2 Hurricane Earl

Also originating off the western coast of Africa as a tropical wave, tropical depression Earl preceded Georges and entered the southwest Gulf of Mexico on August 31, 1998. This tropical depression was upgraded to tropical storm Earl while centered approximately 575 miles (925 km) south-southwest of New Orleans, Louisiana. Earl reached hurricane status on September 2, 1998 while centered 144 miles (232 km) south-southeast of New Orleans. Earl made landfall near Panama City, Florida on September 3, 1998 after attaining a category-two hurricane status.

Unfiltered acoustic backscatter data for this less intense storm were compared to unfiltered current velocity data for the period of September 2-8, 1998. Moorings B2 (29.21°N, 87.87°W) and D1 (30.07°N, 86.84°W) showed a sudden dramatic increase in acoustic backscatter intensity accompanied by abrupt changes in the north/south (v) and east/west (u) current velocity components. These peaks in both backscatter and velocity data were evident from September 2 - 3, 1998 and were most easily recognized in the upper 20m of water. Figures 3.2.2-1 and 3.2.2-2 compare acoustic backscatter intensity with current velocity components at moorings B2 and D1. North/south current velocities ranged from +80 cm/s to -30 cm/s at mooring B2, and velocities ranged from 60 cm/s in the eastward direction to 100 cm/s in the westward direction. Mooring D1 showed current flow alternating from 60 cm/s in the northward direction to 60 cm/s southward, and velocity values ranging from 20 cm/s towards the east and over 100 cm/s towards the west. Unlike the stronger Hurricane Georges, Hurricane Earl was not strong enough to cause abrupt changes in current velocity at mid-water depths. However, mooring D1 did show evidence of increased current velocity throughout the water column (as deep as

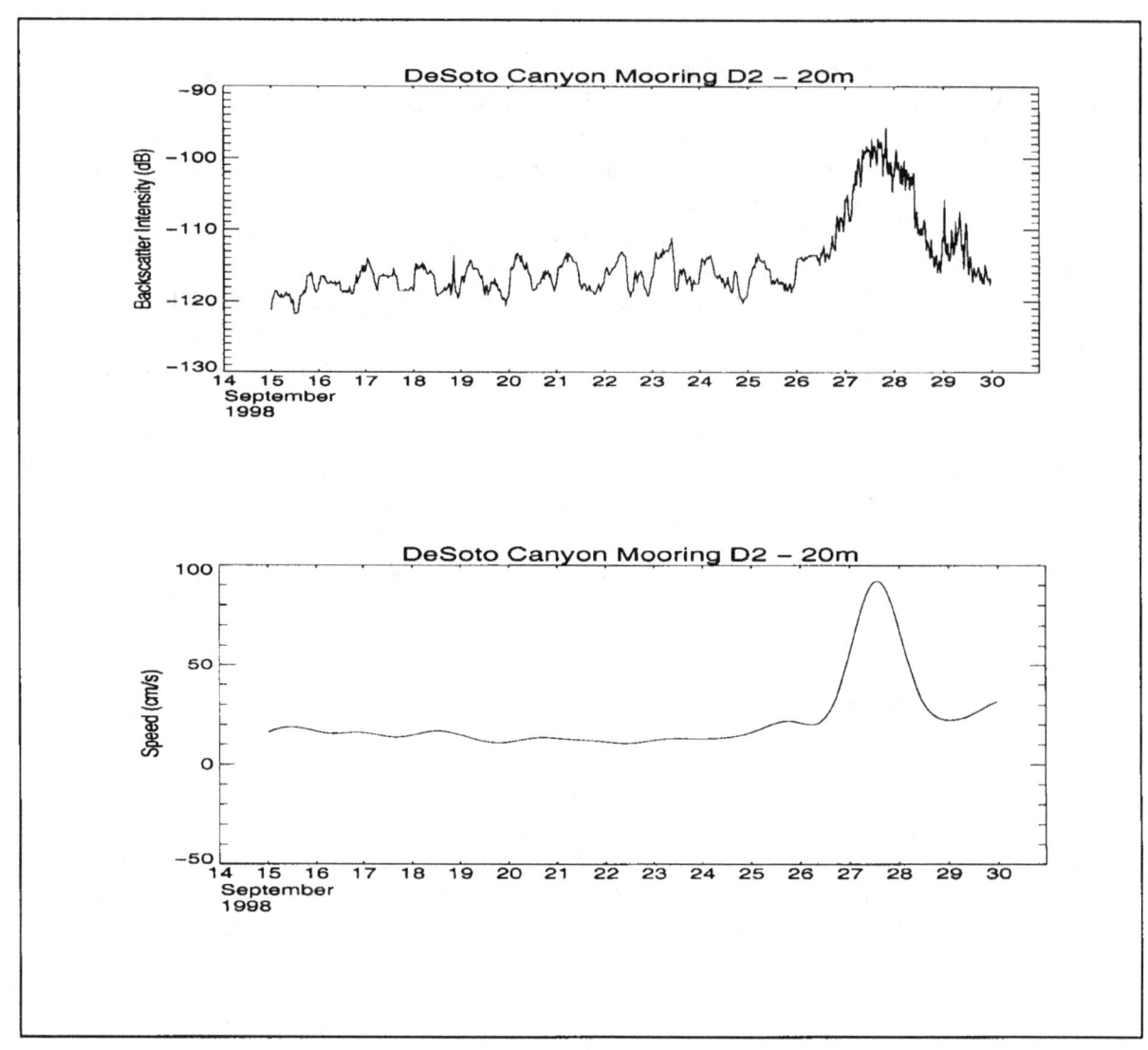

Figure 3.2.1-3. Comparison of unfiltered acoustic backscatter intensity during Hurricane Georges (upper) and filtered current speed during the same time period. Data were taken from 20m depth at mooring D2.

30

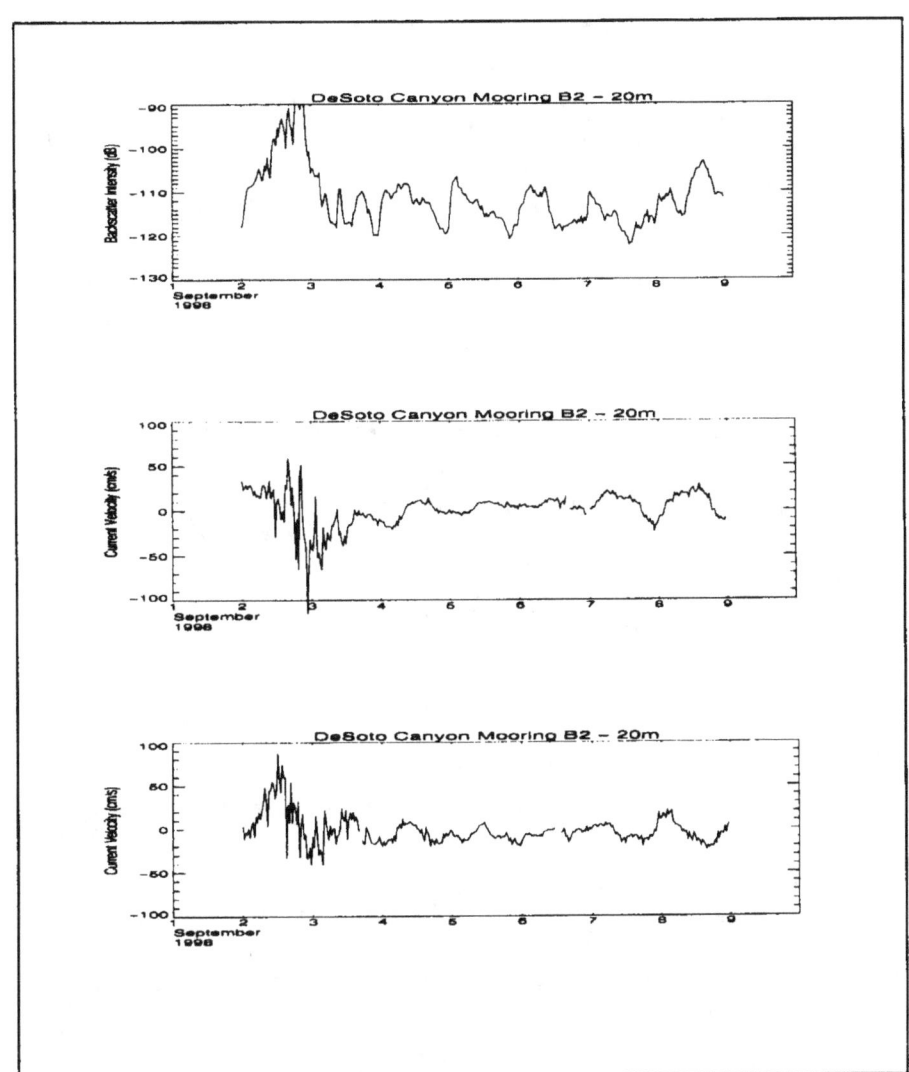

Figure 3.2.2-1. Comparisons between unfiltered acoustic backscatter
intensity and unfiltered current velocity components
during the period of Hurricane Earl. A time series of
acoustic backscatter intensity is given in the upper figure.
The middle figure depicts a time series of the E/W current
velocity component, and the N/S current velocity component
is depicted in the lower figure. Time series were generated
using data from the 20 m depth bin, mooring B2.

31

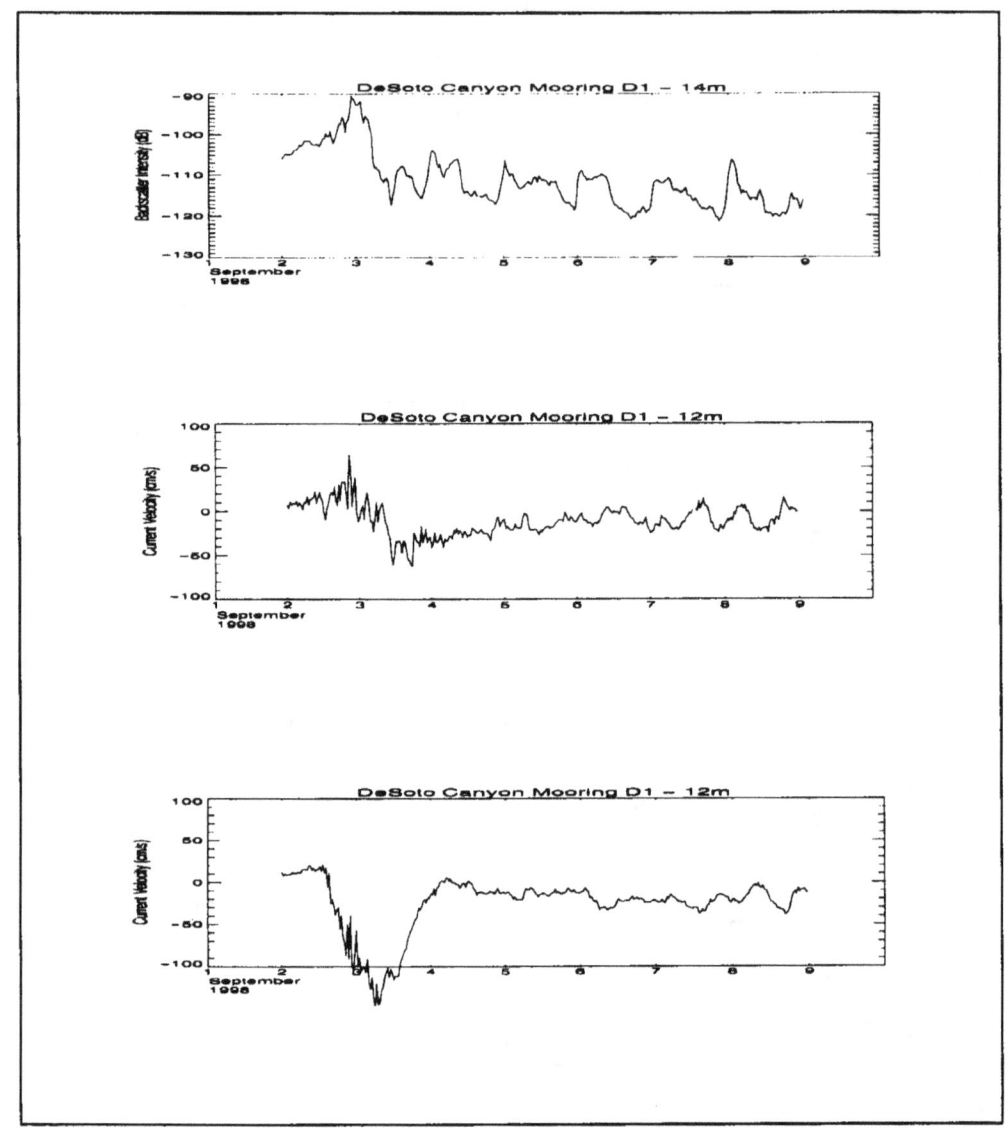

Figure 3.2.2-2. Comparisons between unfiltered acoustic backscatter intensity and unfiltered current velocity components during the period of Hurricane Earl. A time series of backscatter intensity is given in the upper figure. The middle figure depicts a time series of the N/S current velocity component, and the E/W current velocity component is depicted in the lower figure. Time series were generated using data from the uppermost depth bin at mooring D1.

68m). Hurricane Earl was centered approximately 45 miles (72 km) south of mooring D1 on September 3, 1998. Examination of raw acoustic backscatter data for the period of Earl again showed evidence of zooplankton diel vertical migration throughout the water column.

Current speeds were calculated using the u and v current velocity components, and the filtered current speeds were compared to 40-hour low-pass filtered backscatter data. Current speed and backscatter intensity were highly correlated in the upper 20m of water. Figure 3.2.2-3 shows time series of backscatter intensity and current speed recorded during the storm event at mooring D1. For both Hurricanes Georges and Earl, acoustic backscatter intensity and current speed were only highly correlated in the upper 20m of the water column. This implies that wind-induced surface turbulence was responsible for sudden increases in acoustic backscatter during both storms. As explained by Orr et al. (2000), acoustic signals may be scattered by sharp changes in temperature and salinity associated with oceanic mixing events. Abrupt changes in acoustic scattering can also occur in high shear zones, when bubbles are mixed downward from surface turbulence, or when wave action and breaking occur (DiMarco et al. 1995; Orr et al. 2000). Although current velocities were elevated throughout the water column during Hurricane Georges, the downward mixing of bubbles was apparently not strong enough to produce changes in acoustic backscatter intensity below 20m. This observation is consistent with results published by DiMarco et al. (1995) which showed that significant wave heights during hurricane events in the Gulf of Mexico did not exceed 10m.

3.3 Acoustic Backscatter and Ocean Color

Ocean color data are important components in the study of ocean primary production and global biogeochemistry. Ocean color varies with the concentration of chlorophyll and other plant pigments present in the water, and phytoplankton concentrations can be derived from quantification of ocean color seen in satellite observations. As a continuation of the Coastal Zone Color Scanner (CZCS) project, the Sea Wide Field-of-view Sensor (SeaWiFS) Project provides quantitative data on global ocean bio-optical properties (Behrenfield et al. 2001). This Earth-orbiting ocean color sensor collects ocean color data used for estimating global standing stocks of ocean phytoplankton.

The average chlorophyll value at each of the ADCP mooring locations was extracted from the 52 biweekly intervals (104 weeks) of the 1998-1999 data series. This average chlorophyll value for each of the moorings was calculated as the mean of a five pixel by five pixel grid centered on the specified latitude/longitude location of each of the ADCP moorings. Each SeaWiFs pixel has 2.8 x 4.1 km resolution, so the effective area around each ADCP mooring that was averaged at each biweekly interval equaled 287 km^2.

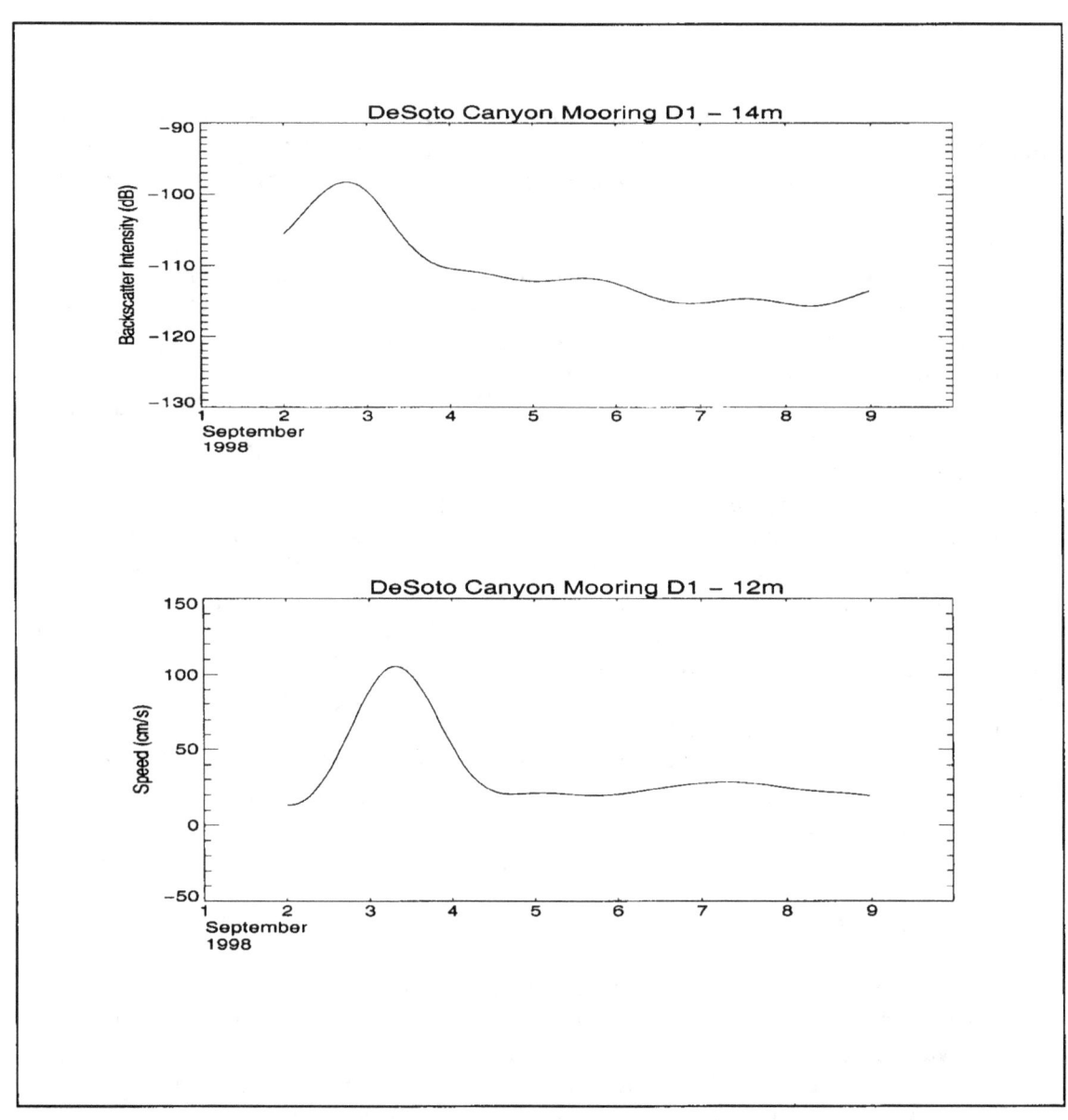

Figure 3.2.2-3. Comparison of filtered acoustic backscatter intensity during Hurricane Earl (upper) and filtered current speed during the same time period (lower). Data were taken from the uppermost depth bin at mooring D1.

Figure 3.3-1 shows the average chlorophyll concentration as determined from SeaWiFS data at each of the 12 ADCP moorings. Mean chlorophyll concentrations were highest near the mouth of the Mississippi River (moorings A1, A2, A3) and decreased as the distance between the moorings and river region increased. The biweekly data reveal that chlorophyll concentrations were generally highest (24 mg/m^3) during the period extending from late May through late July 1998 (biweekly intervals 11-15). Lowest chlorophyll concentrations occurred from early October through mid December 1998 (biweekly intervals 21-25). To investigate the relationship between SeaWiFS chlorophyll values and acoustic backscatter intensity data, an average backscatter intensity value was calculated using data from the uppermost depth bin at each of the moored ADCPs. Backscatter intensity data were averaged over the two ten-week periods (biweekly intervals 11-15 and 21-25) corresponding to highest and lowest chlorophyll concentration values.

A Spearman Rank Correlation test was used to define the relationship between acoustic backscatter intensity and chlorophyll concentrations in the northeastern Gulf of Mexico. The standard correlation coefficient, r, determines the linear relationship between two variables x and y, but the rank correlation coefficient measures whether y increases or decreases with x even when the relationship is not necessarily linear. All x and y values are ranked individually, and the standard correlation coefficient is calculated for the ranks. This test was conducted using ten backscatter/chlorophyll data pairs (n = 10) corresponding to biweekly intervals 11-15 and 21-25. With a calculated correlation coefficient $r_s = 0.84$, there was a robust positive correlation between acoustic backscatter and chlorophyll significant at the 0.01 significance level.

Ocean color research in the Gulf of Mexico has enabled the description of seasonal variations in phytoplankton concentrations, yet SeaWiFS chlorophyll data used in this study were sharply out of phase with typical deep water annual cycles. The well-defined annual cycle of phytoplankton concentrations in the Gulf is characterized by distinct periods of high and low pigment concentrations. Highest concentrations (>0.18 mg/m^3) occur between December and February, while lowest concentrations (~0.06 mg/m^3) are generally seen between May and July. Mixed layer depth is the most important controlling factor for this annual cycle (Muller-Karger et al. 1991), but eddy presence also affects the cycle. During the present study warm slope eddies persisted in the DeSoto Canyon area from May through August in both 1997 and 1998. Specifically, analysis of SSHA plots revealed the presence of a large anticyclonic eddy (Eddy Gyre) persistent over the study area during the summer of 1998. As nutrient-rich Mississippi River water enters the Gulf, productivity increases near the mouth of the river and phytoplankton blooms occur. Physical features such as Eddy Gyre entrain this low salinity, high chlorophyll water from the Mississippi River and transport it seaward. This entrainment of "green water" from the Mississippi River appears to have been responsible for the high summer time ocean color that was out of phase with the typical annual cycle.

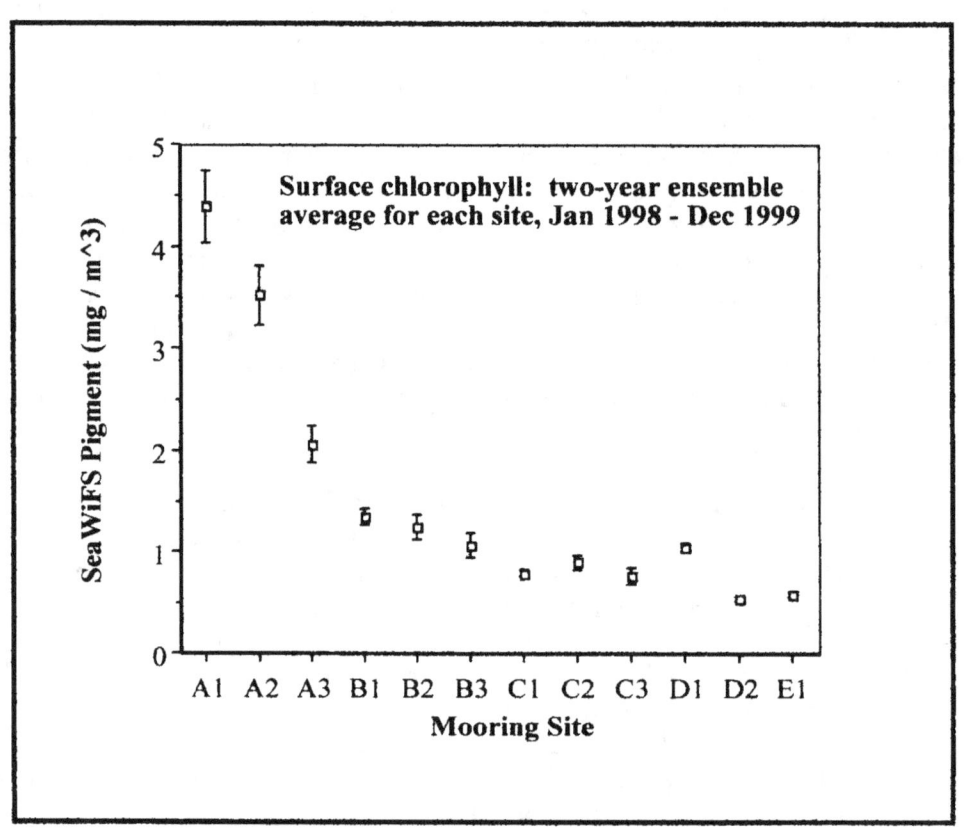

Figure 3.3-1. Box and whisker plot showing the two-year average surface chlorophyll concentration at each of the 12 mooring locations. Boxes show the two-year mean and whiskers show the standard error of the mean.

Shipboard measurements of chlorophyll fluorescence that were logged every two minutes during NEGOM cruises N3 and N6 confirmed that most of the ocean color signal was the result of chlorophyll-a (Jochens and Nowlin 1998; Jochens and Nowlin 1999). However, concurrent fluoremetric measurements of colored dissolved organic matter (CDOM) made with a second flow-through fluorometer documented that 'gelbstoff' contributed to the ocean color signal as well, especially in the core of the green water river plume (Hu et al. 2001).

4.0 **Summary and Conclusions**

Analysis of combined acoustic backscatter intensity data from a moored array of ADCPs and zooplankton collections made in the northeastern Gulf of Mexico enabled us to conclude that backscatter data recorded by ADCPs does represent a biological signal directly related to the size and concentration of zooplankton in the water column. Regression analysis showed a positive relationship between acoustic backscatter intensity and zooplankton biomass, and the power of this relationship was higher for large-size organisms (> 2 mm). Vertical analysis of ABI in the upper 90m of the water column revealed a general increase in backscatter with increasing depth. This result was not unexpected, as plankton are not evenly distributed vertically. Herbivorous zooplankton are usually more abundant at or near the DCM, which is usually deeper than 70m in the Gulf of Mexico. Through spatial backscatter analysis we found that mean backscatter intensity for the two-year record was highest at the shelf-break sites and lowest at oceanic stations. Again these results were not unexpected, for as do other oceans, the Gulf of Mexico has higher plankton stocks in neritic than oceanic waters.

In an effort to better understand the relationship between acoustic backscatter intensity and chlorophyll concentrations in the northeastern Gulf of Mexico, backscatter data were used in conjunction with SeaWiFS ocean color data from the study area. We found a significant positive correlation between acoustic backscatter intensity and chlorophyll concentrations. These results were not surprising, as zooplankton populations increase with enhanced food supply. However, chlorophyll concentrations did not follow the well-defined annual cycle of primary production for the Gulf of Mexico, and analysis of SSHA plots showed that this was due to the entrainment of low salinity, high chlorophyll river water by warm slope eddies located over the study area.

Spectral analysis of acoustic time series data allowed us to study the variance in acoustic backscatter intensity as a function of frequency. Evident in all plotted spectra was a sharp peak in energy density centered at one cycle per day, and these peaks were indicative of the diel vertical migration of zooplankton in the water column. All plotted spectra were red, showing decreases in spectral density as frequency increased. Red variance spectra are common for oceanic long-term variability, and this spectral analysis revealed low-frequency, weekly to monthly variability in the backscatter record associated with current flow in the DeSoto Canyon area.

To further investigate the relationship between acoustic backscatter intensity and current flow, correlation analysis was carried out using combined backscatter and current velocity data. Significant correlations between acoustic backscatter intensity and off-shore flow indicated the transport of neritic zooplankton off shore to deeper waters. Backscatter intensity was also correlated with along-shelf flow, although these correlations varied as the direction of flow changed relative to the along-margin movement of mesoscale physical features.

The effect of hurricane-strength mixing events on backscatter intensity was investigated using data from Hurricanes Georges and Earl, and it was found that there is a backscatter response to such storm events. However, the response in backscatter intensity is most likely not a biological response. Rather, the response is a physical consequence of the abrupt changes in acoustic scattering that occur with the downward mixing of bubbles from surface turbulence and wave action and breaking.

5.0 **References**

Behrenfeld, M.J., J.T. Randerson, C.R. McClain, G.C. Feldman, S.O. Los, C.J. Tucker, P.G. Falkowski, C.B. Field, R. Frouin, W.E. Esaias, D.D. Kolber, and N.H. Pollack. 2001. Biospheric primary production during ENSO transition. Science 291, 2594-2597.

Brierley, A.S., M.A. Brandon, and J.L. Watkins. 1998. An assessment of the utility of an acoustic Doppler current profiler for biomass estimation. Deep-Sea Research I 45(9): 1555-1573.

Capurro, L.R.A. and J.L. Reid (eds.). 1972. Contributions on the physical oceanography of the Gulf of Mexico. Houston, TX: Gulf Publishing Company. 288 pp.

Deines, K.L. 1999. Backscatter estimation using broadband acoustic Doppler current profilers. In: Anderson, S.P. et al. (eds.). Proceedings of the IEEE Sixth Working Conference on Current Measurement, March 11-13, 1999. Pp. 249-253.

DiMarco, S.F., F.J. Kelly, J. Zhang, and N.L. Guinasso, Jr. 1995. Directional wave spectra on the Louisiana-Texas shelf during Hurricane Andrew. Journal of Coastal Research, Special Issue No. 21: 217-233.

Emery, W.J. and R.E. Thomson. 1997. Data analysis methods in physical oceanography. Kidlington, NY. 634 pp.

Flagg, C.N. and S.L. Smith. 1989. On the use of the acoustic Doppler current profiler to measure zooplankton abundance. Deep-Sea Research I 36(3): 455-474.

Gordon, R.L. 1996. Acoustic Doppler current profilers- principles of operation: A practical primer. RD Instruments, San Diego, CA. 54 pp.

Greene, C.H. and P.H. Wiebe. 1990. Bioacoustical oceanography: new tools for zooplankton and micronekton research in the 1990s. Oceanography 3(1): 12-17.

Griffiths, G. and J.I. Diaz. 1996. Comparison of acoustic backscatter from a ship-mounted acoustic Doppler current profiler and an EK500 scientific echosounder. ICES Journal of Marine Science 53: 487-491.

Hamilton, P. 1999. DeSoto Canyon circulation and exchange. Physical/Biological Oceanographic Integration Workshop, U.S. Minerals Management Service. Mobile, AL, October 19, 1999.

Hamilton, P., T.J. Berger, J.J. Singer, E. Waddell, J.H. Churchill, R.R. Leben, T.N. Lee, and W. Sturges. 2000. DeSoto Canyon Eddy Intrusion Study; Final Report in two volumes (Vol. 1: Executive Summary; Vol. 2: Technical Report). OCS Study MMS 2000-079 (Vol. 1, 37 pp.) and MMS 2000-080 (Vol. 2, 275 pp.). U.S. Dept. of the Interior, Minerals Management Service, Gulf of Mexico OCS Region, New Orleans, LA.

Heywood, K.J., S. Scrope-Howe, and E.D. Barton. 1991. Estimation of zooplankton abundance from shipborne ADCP backscatter. Deep-Sea Research I 38(6): 677-691.

Hoffmann, E.E. and S.J. Worley. 1986. An investigation of the circulation of the Gulf of Mexico. Journal of Geophysical Research 91(C12): 14221-14236.

Hu, C., F.E. Muller-Karger, D.C. Biggs, K.L. Carder, B. Nababan, D. Nadeau, and J. Vanderbloemen. 2001. Comparison of ship and satellite bio-optical measurements on the continental margin of the NE Gulf of Mexico. International Journal of Remote Sensing, in press.

Jochens, A.E. and W.D. Nowlin, Jr., (eds.), 1998. Northeastern Gulf of Mexico chemical oceanography and hydrography study between the Mississippi delta and Tampa Bay, Annual Report: Year 1. OCS Study MMS 98-0060. U.S. Dept. of the Interior, Minerals Management Service, Gulf of Mexico OCS Region, New Orleans, LA. 126 pp.

Jochens, A.E. and W.D. Nowlin, Jr., (eds.). 1999. Northeastern Gulf of Mexico chemical oceanography and hydrography study: Year 2 - Annual Report. OCS Study MMS 99-0054. U.S. Dept. of the Interior, Minerals Management Service, Gulf of Mexico OCS Region, New Orleans, LA. 123 pp.

Muller-Karger, F.E., J.J. Walsh, R.H. Evans, and M.B. Meyers. 1991. On the seasonal phytoplankton concentration and sea surface temperature cycles of the Gulf of Mexico as determined by satellites. Journal of Geophysical Research 96(C7): 12645-12665.

Nowlin, Jr., W.D., A.E. Jochens, M.K. Howard, and S.F. DiMarco. 2000. Hydrographic properties and inferred circulation over the Northeastern shelves of the Gulf of Mexico during spring to midsummer of 1998. Gulf of Mexico Science 18(1): 40-54.

Nowlin, Jr., W.D., A.E. Jochens, S.F. DiMarco, S.F, R.O. Reid and M.K. Howard. 2001 (in preparation). Deep water physical oceanography reanalysis and synthesis of historical data: Synthesis Report. U.S. Dept. of the Interior Minerals Management Service, Gulf of Mexico OCS Region, New Orleans, LA. 530 pp.

Orr, M.H., L.R. Haury, P.H. Wiebe, and M.G. Briscoe. 2000. Backscatter of high-frequency (200 kHz) acoustic wavefields from ocean turbulence. Journal of the Acoustical Society of America 108(4): 1595-1601.

Rippeth, T.P. and J.H. Simpson. 1998. Diurnal signals in vertical motions on the Hebridean Shelf. Limnology and Oceanography 43: 1690-1696.

Roe, H.S.J. and G. Griffiths. 1992. Biological information from an acoustic Doppler current profiler. Marine Biology 115: 339-346.

Smith, P.E., M.D. Ohman, and L.E. Eber. 1989. Analysis of the patterns of distribution of zooplankton aggregations from an acoustic Doppler current profiler. California Cooperative Oceanic Fisheries Investigations Reports 30: 88-103.

Sturges, W. and R. Leben. 2000. Frequency of ring separations from the Loop Current in the Gulf of Mexico: a revised estimate. Journal of Physical Oceanography 30: 1814-1819.

Woodward, W.E. and G.F. Appell. 1986. Current velocity measurements using acoustic Doppler backscatter: a review. IEEE Journal of Ocean Engineering 11: 3-6.

Wormuth, J.H., P.H. Ressler, R.B. Cady, and E.J. Harris. 2000. Zooplankton and micronekton in cyclones and anticyclones in the northeast Gulf of Mexico. Gulf of Mexico Science 18: 23-34.

Zimmerman, R.R. and D.C. Biggs. 1999. Patterns of distribution of sound-scattering zooplankton in warm- and cold-core eddies in the Gulf of Mexico, from a narrowband acoustic Doppler current profiler survey. Journal of Geophysical Research 104: 5251-5262.

APPENDIX A:

**Time series of 40-hour low-pass filtered acoustic backscatter intensity.
The two records per panel were selected to illustrate near-surface conditions,
near-instrument conditions, and conditions between these two regions of the water column.**

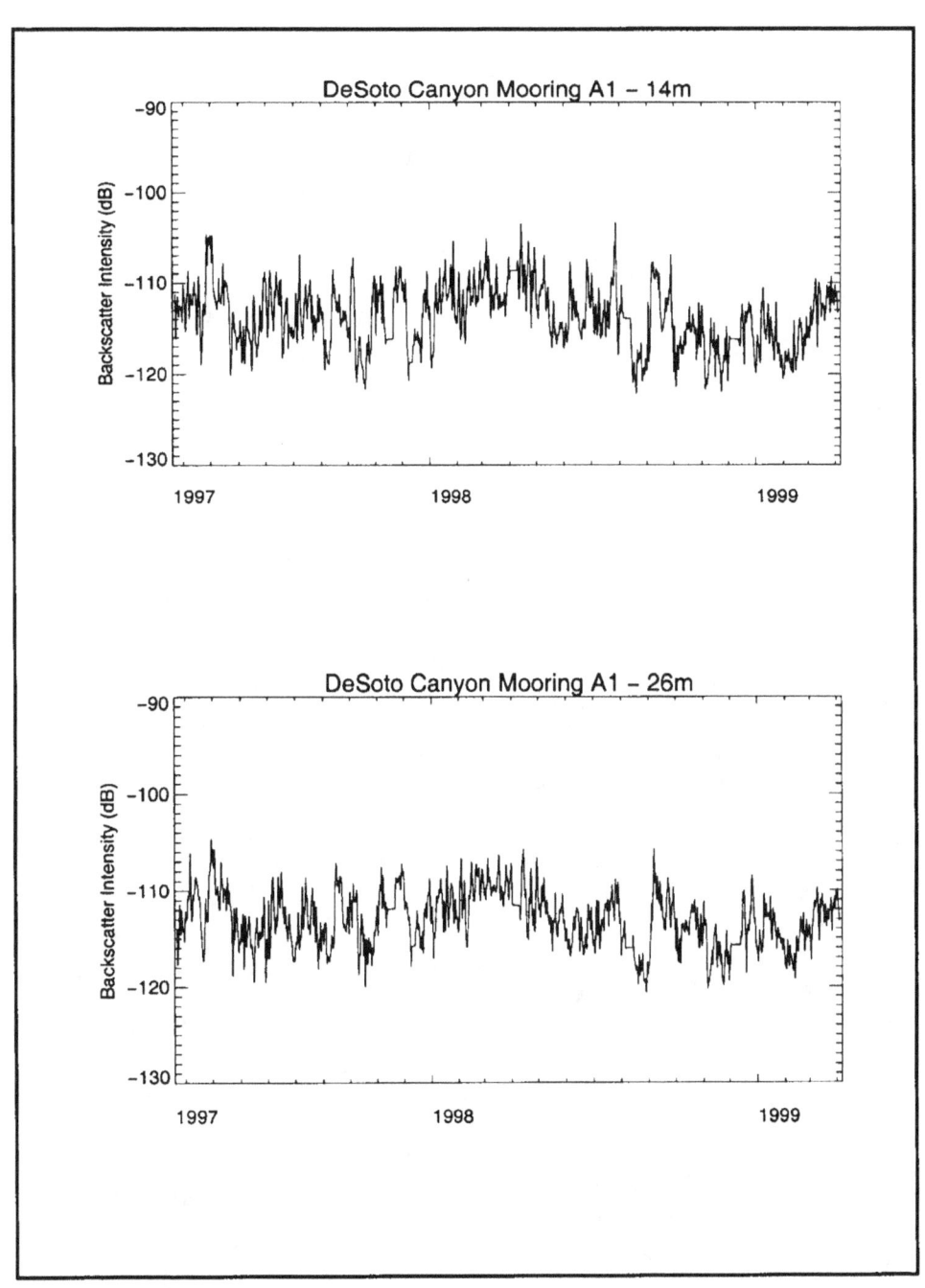

45

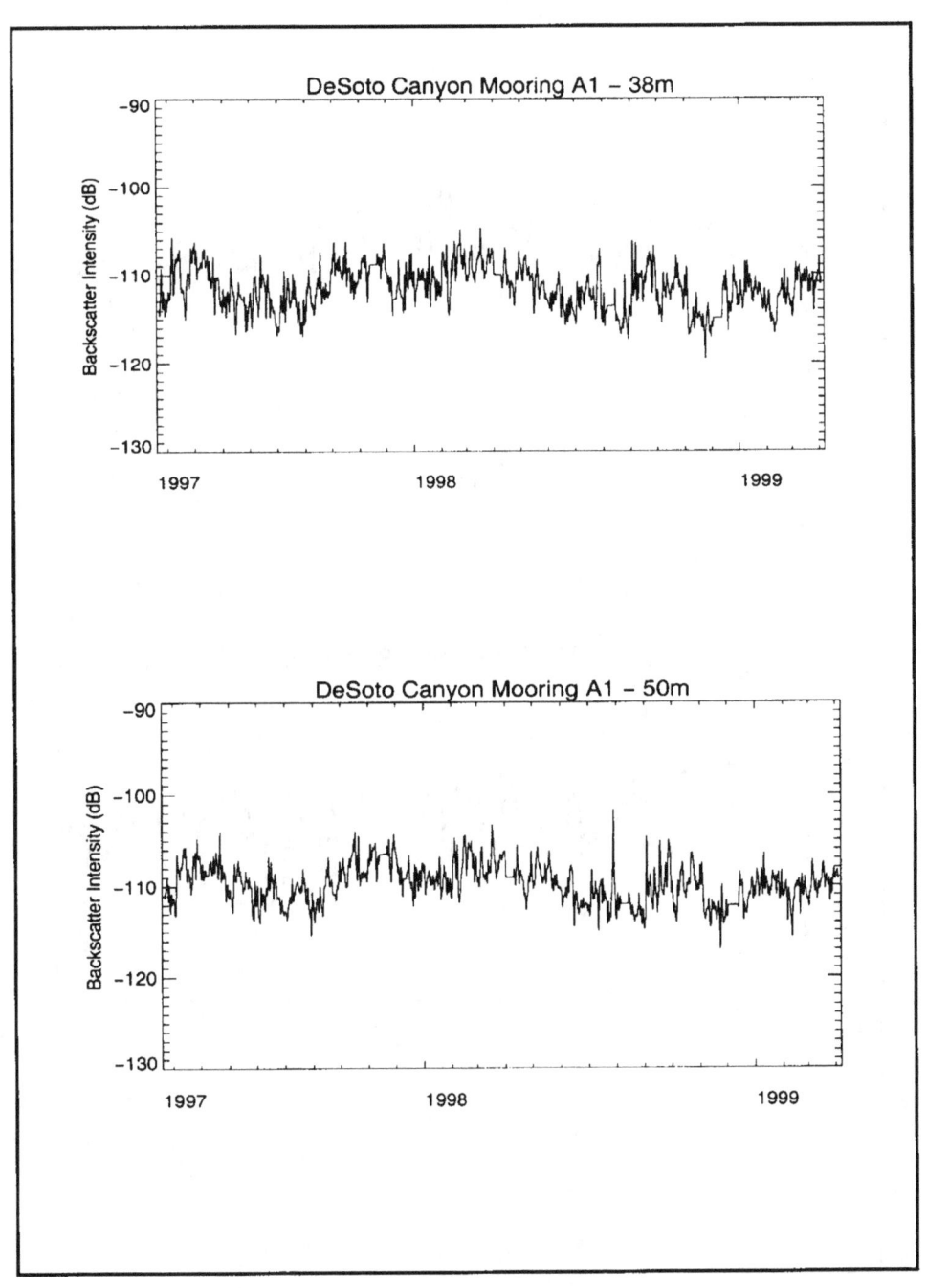

47

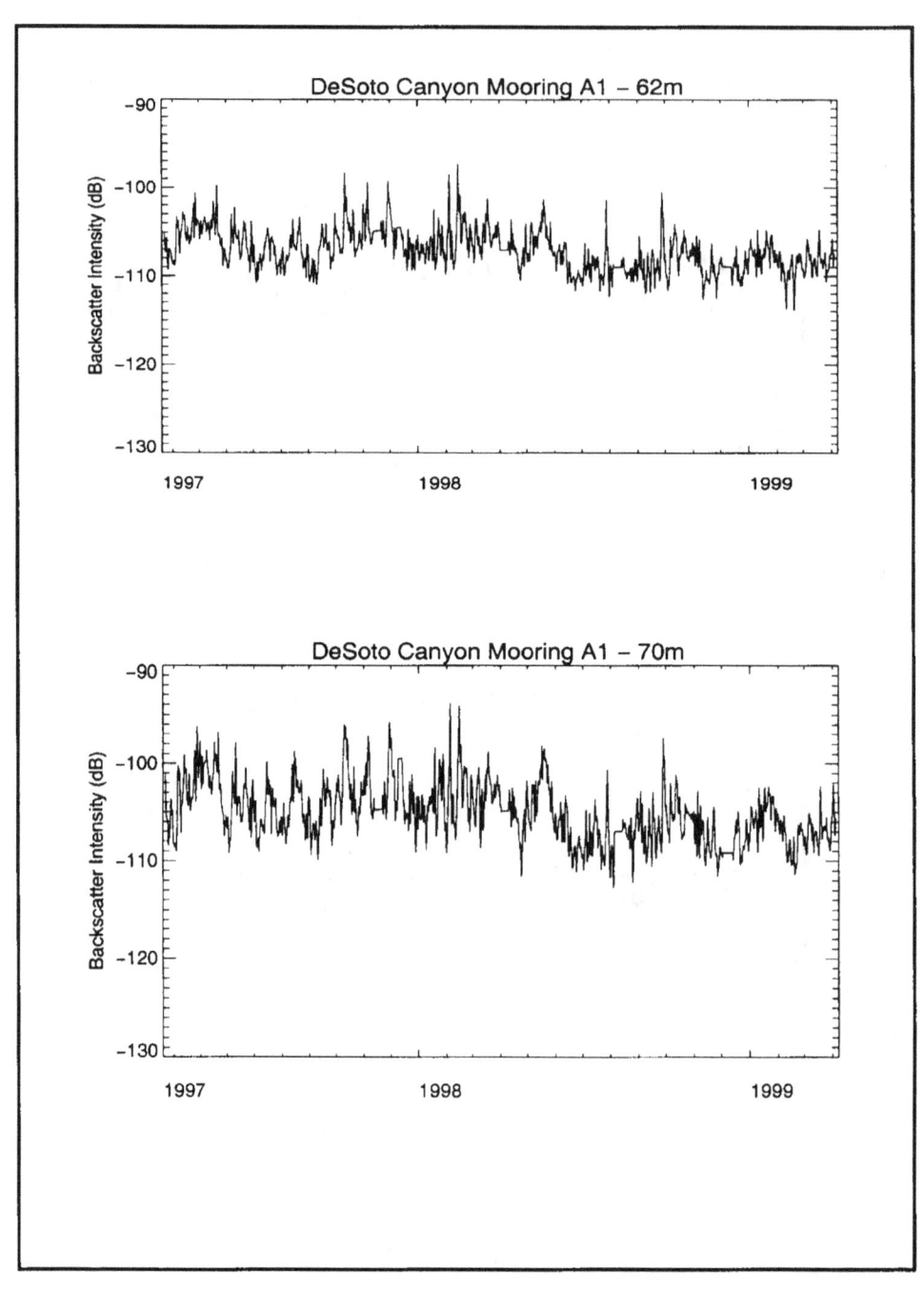

48

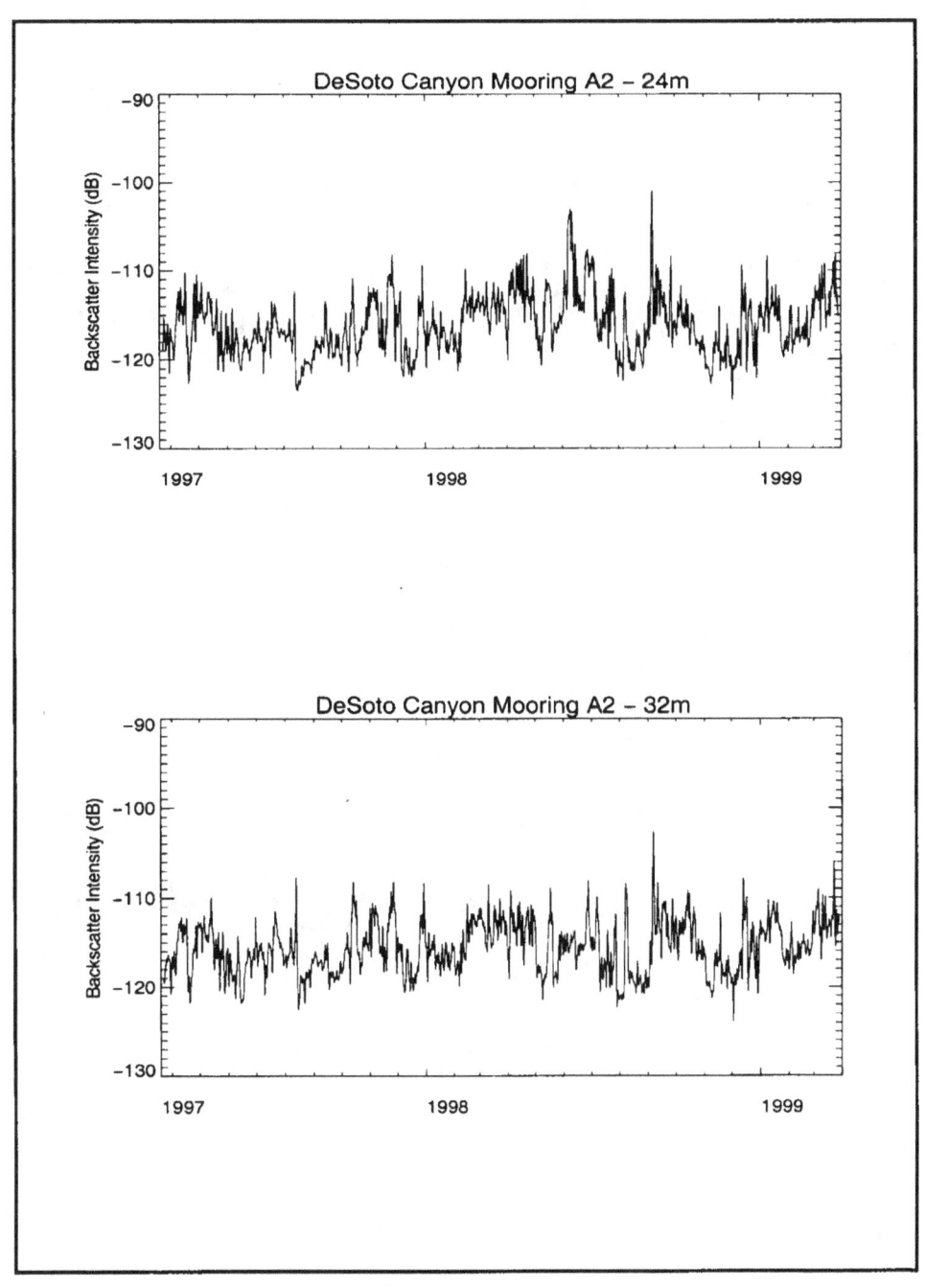

49

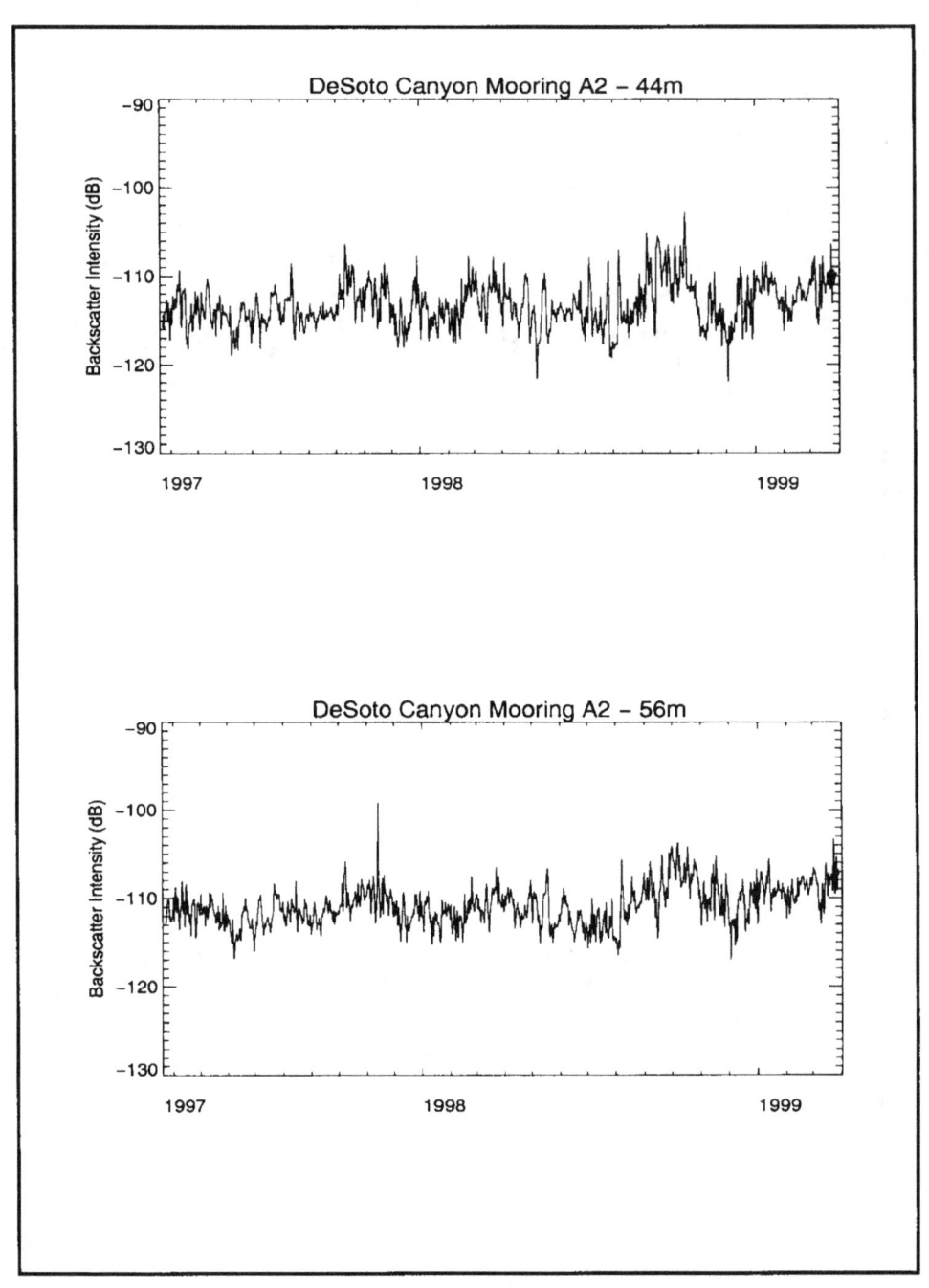

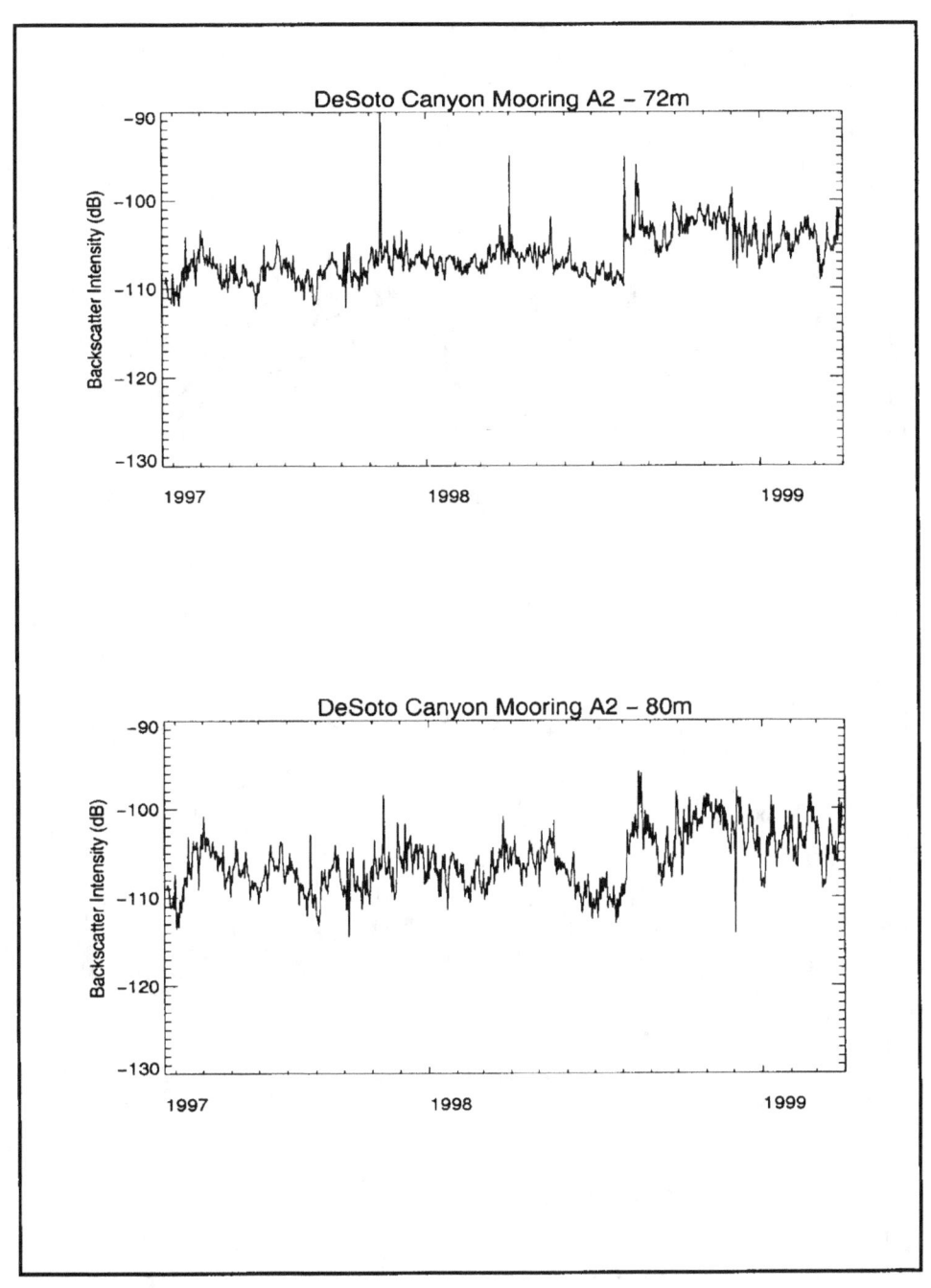

51

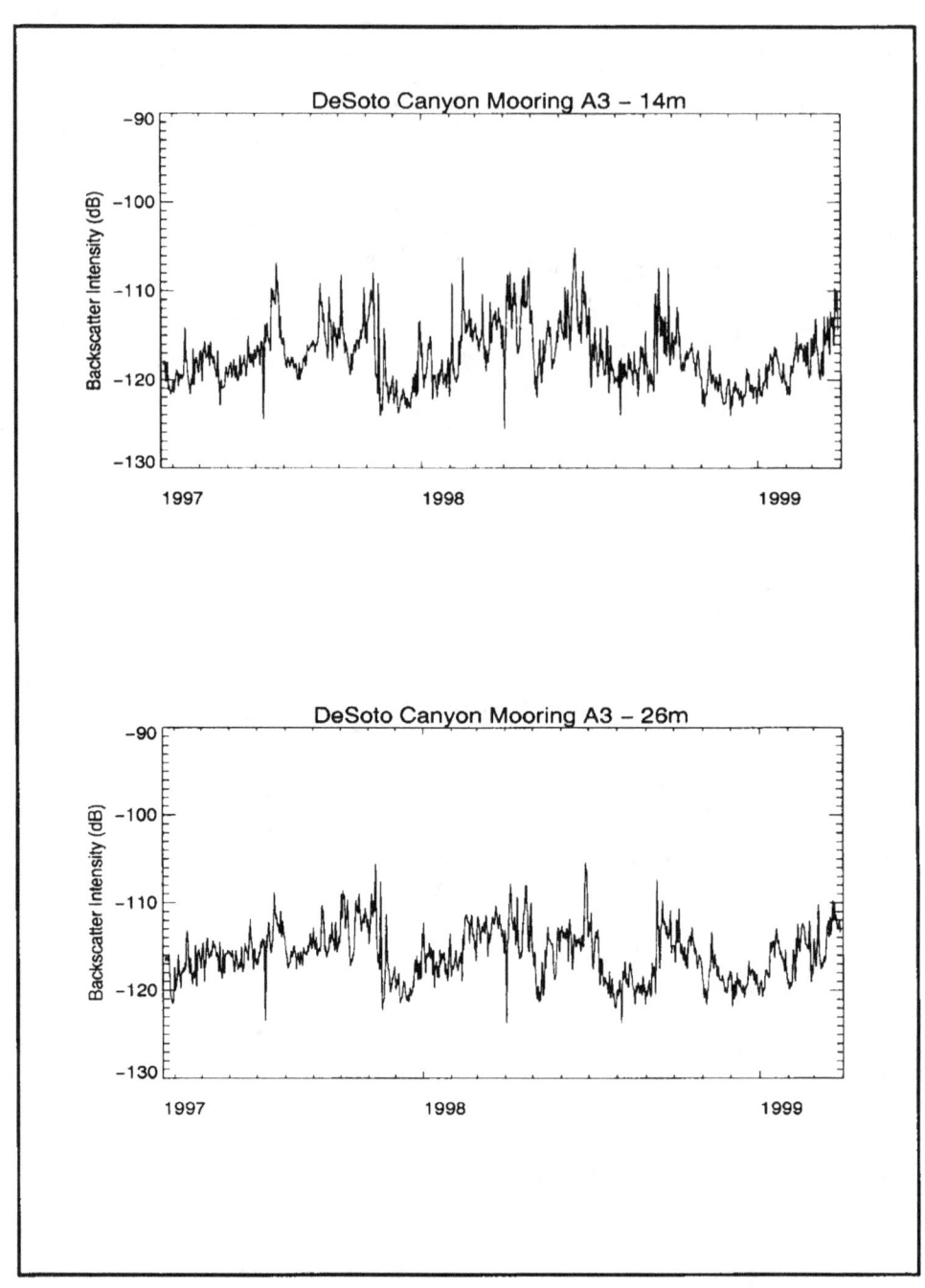

52

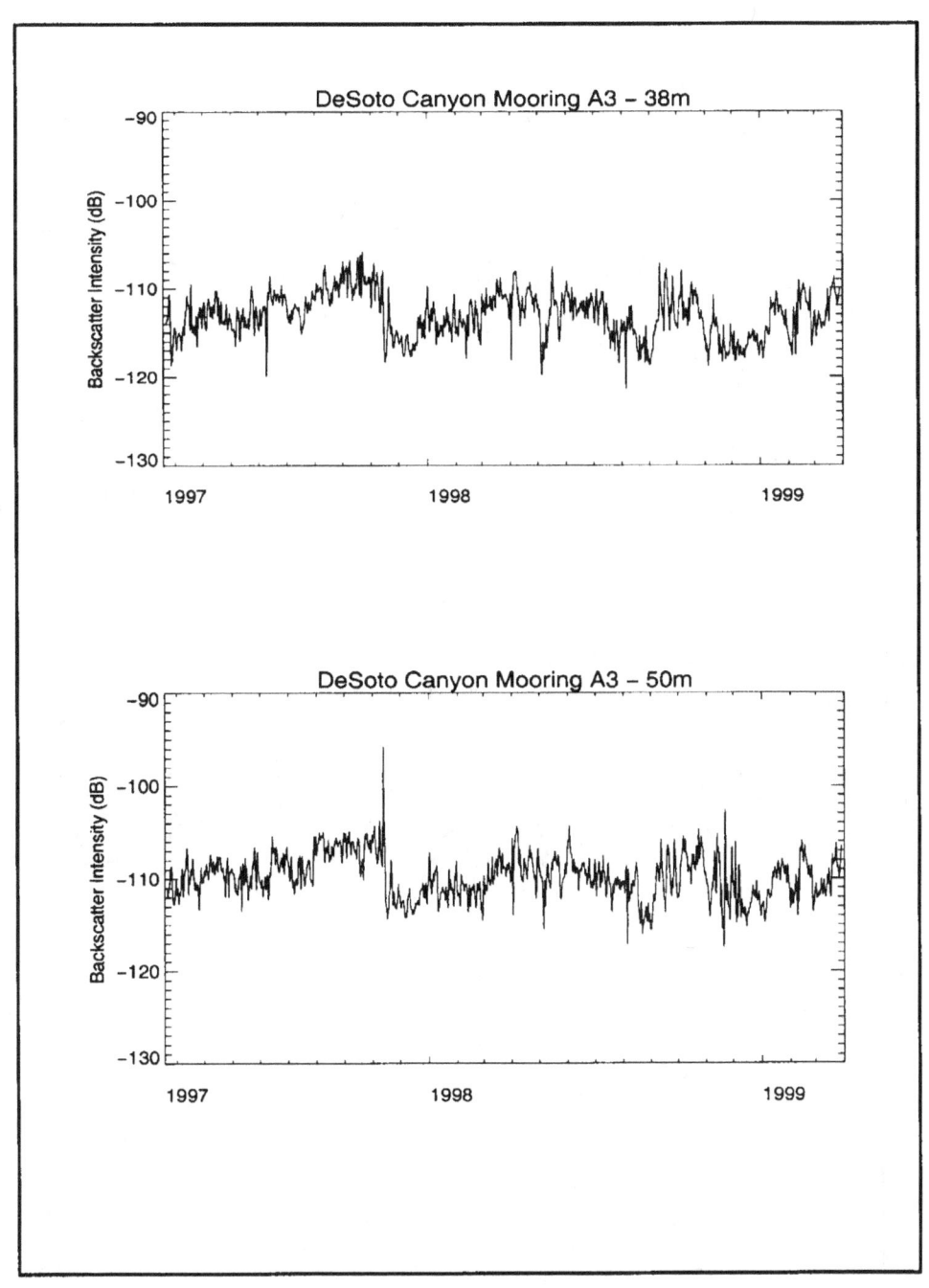

53

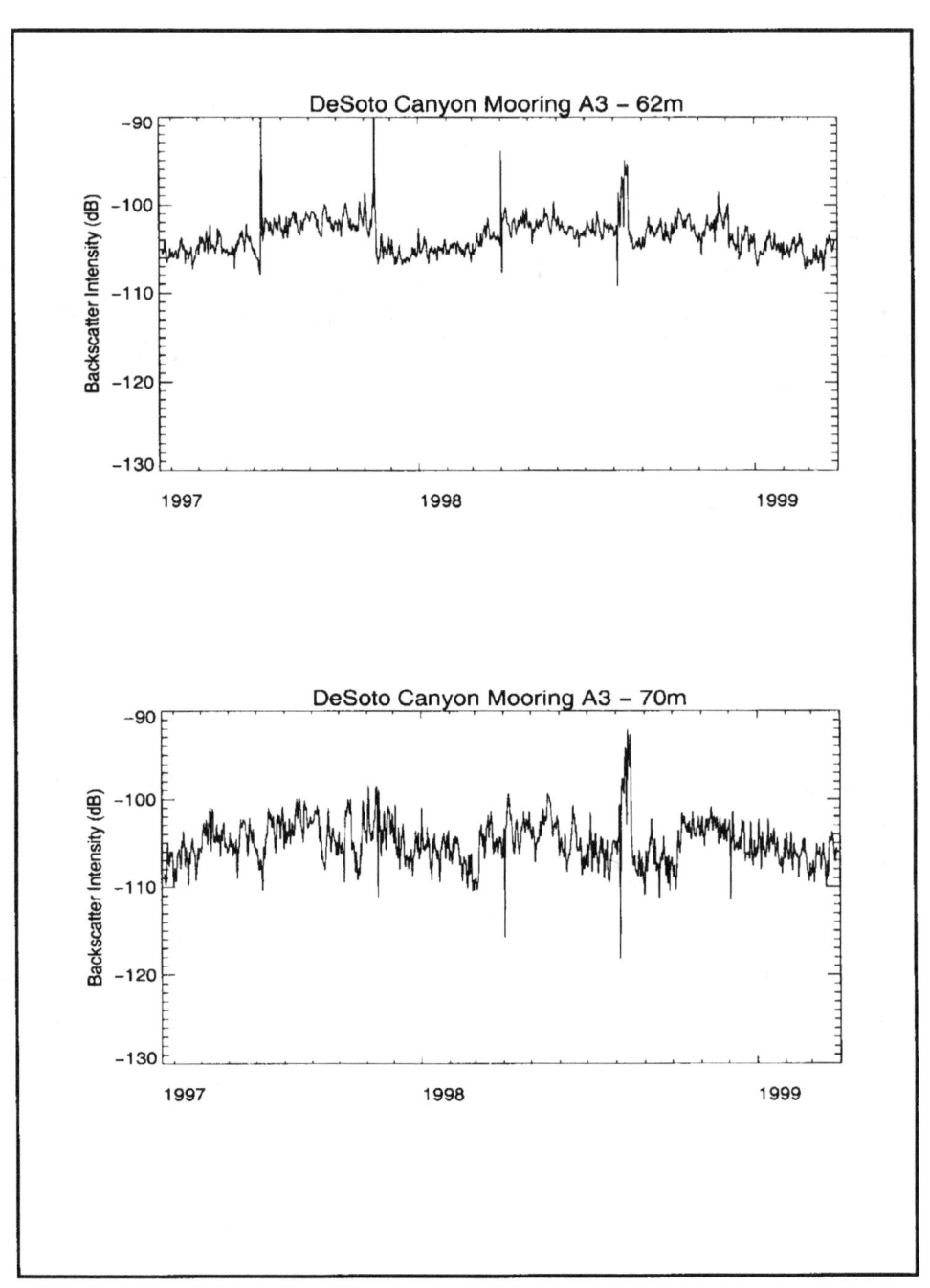

54

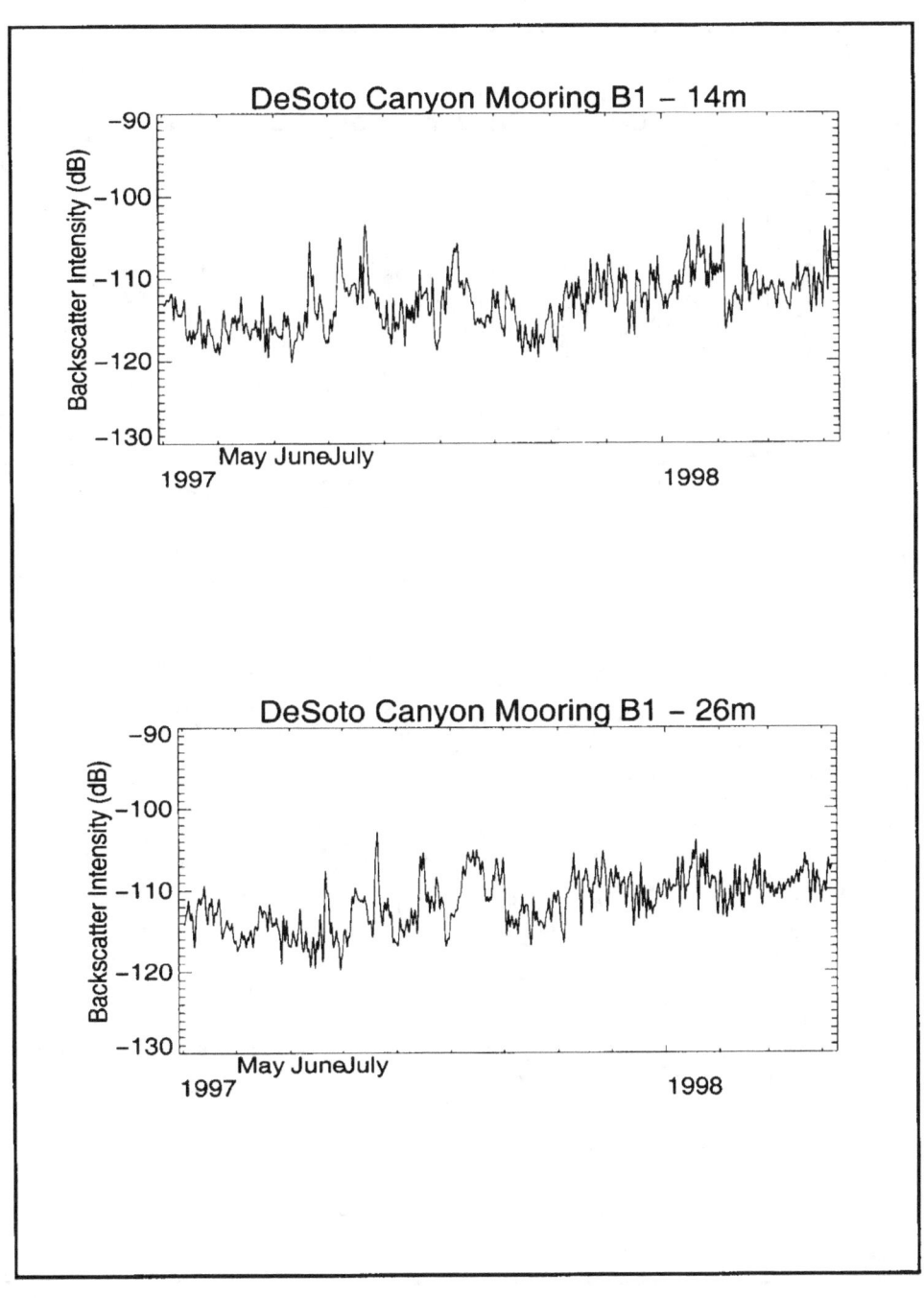

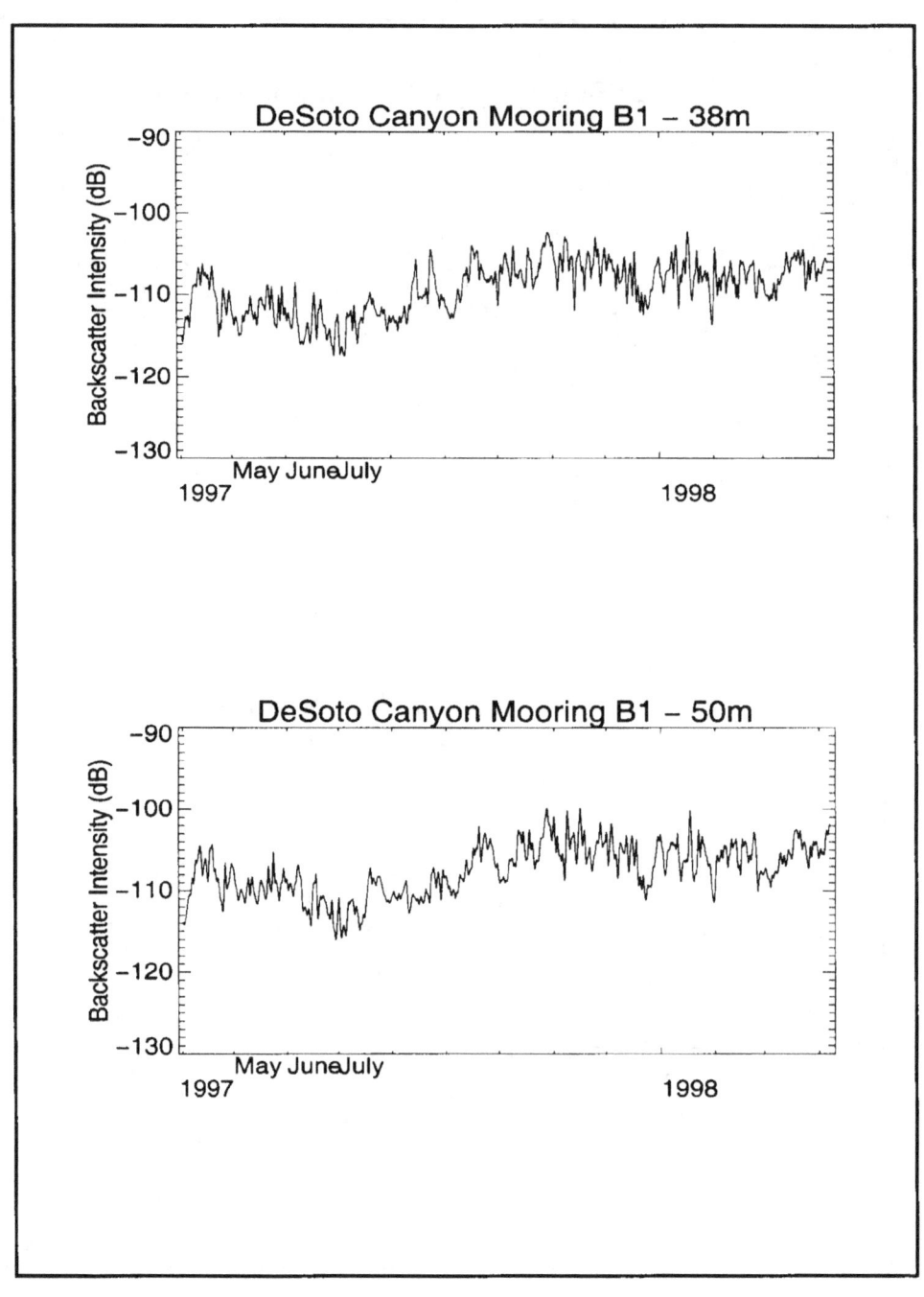

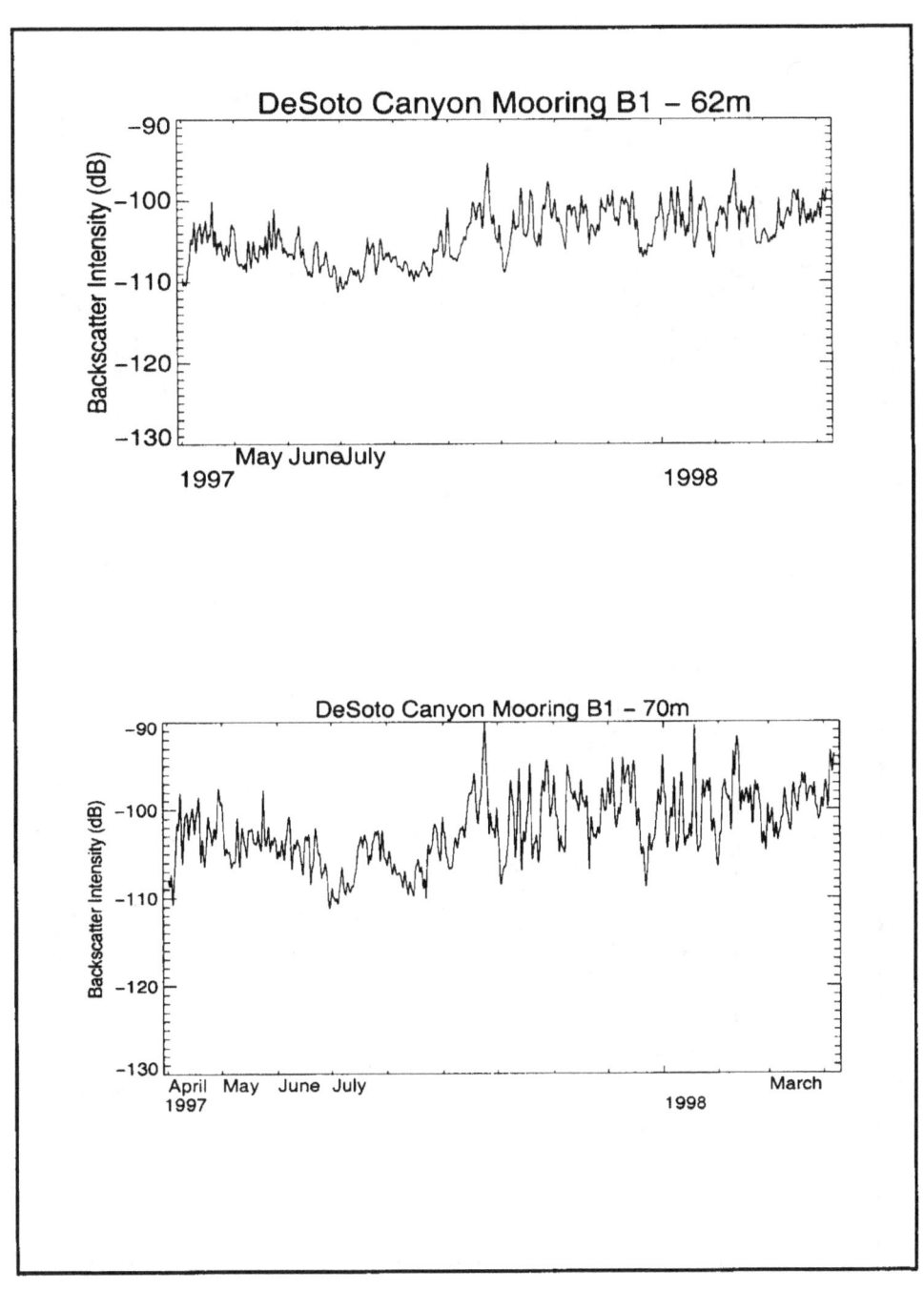

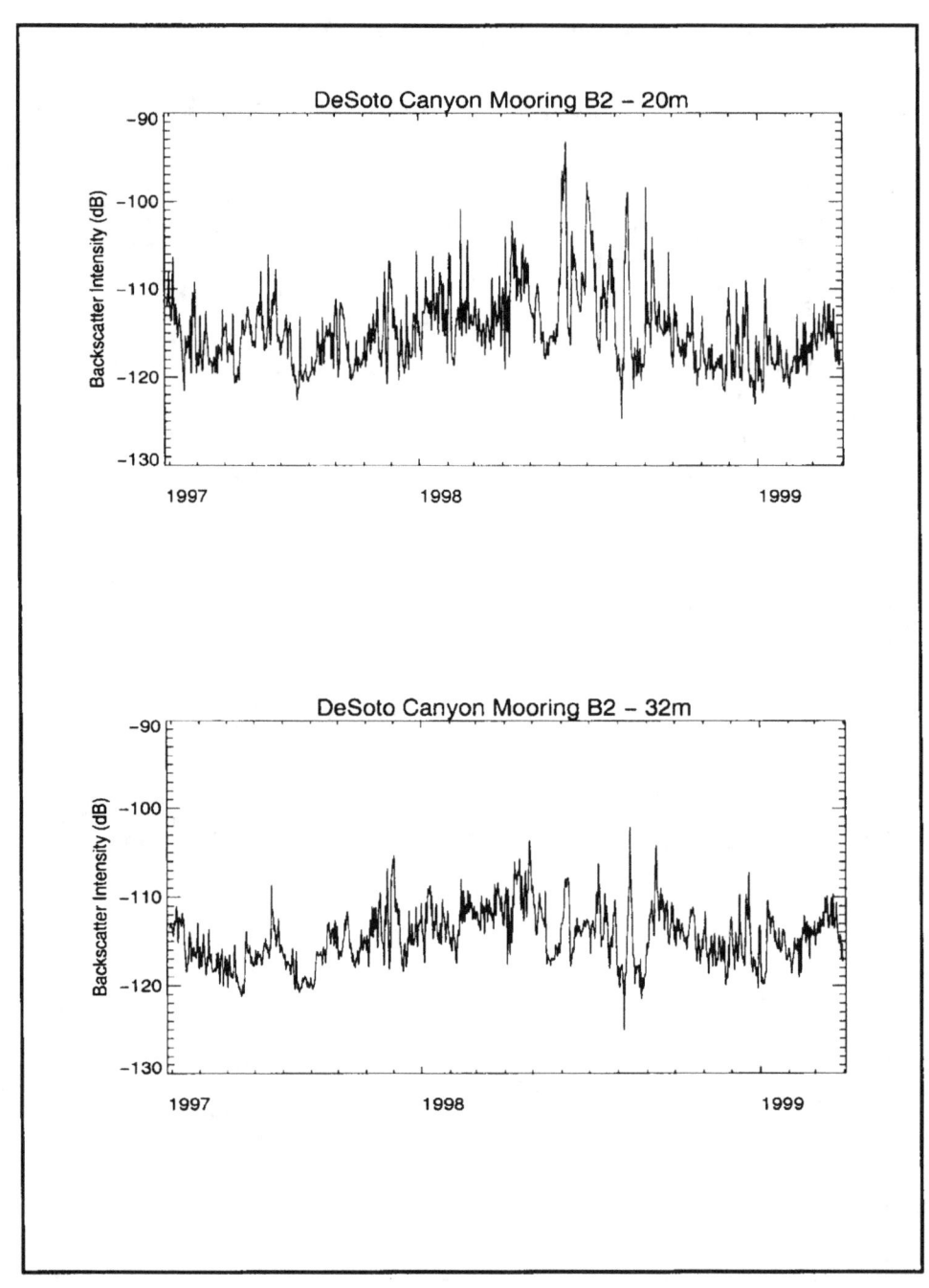

58

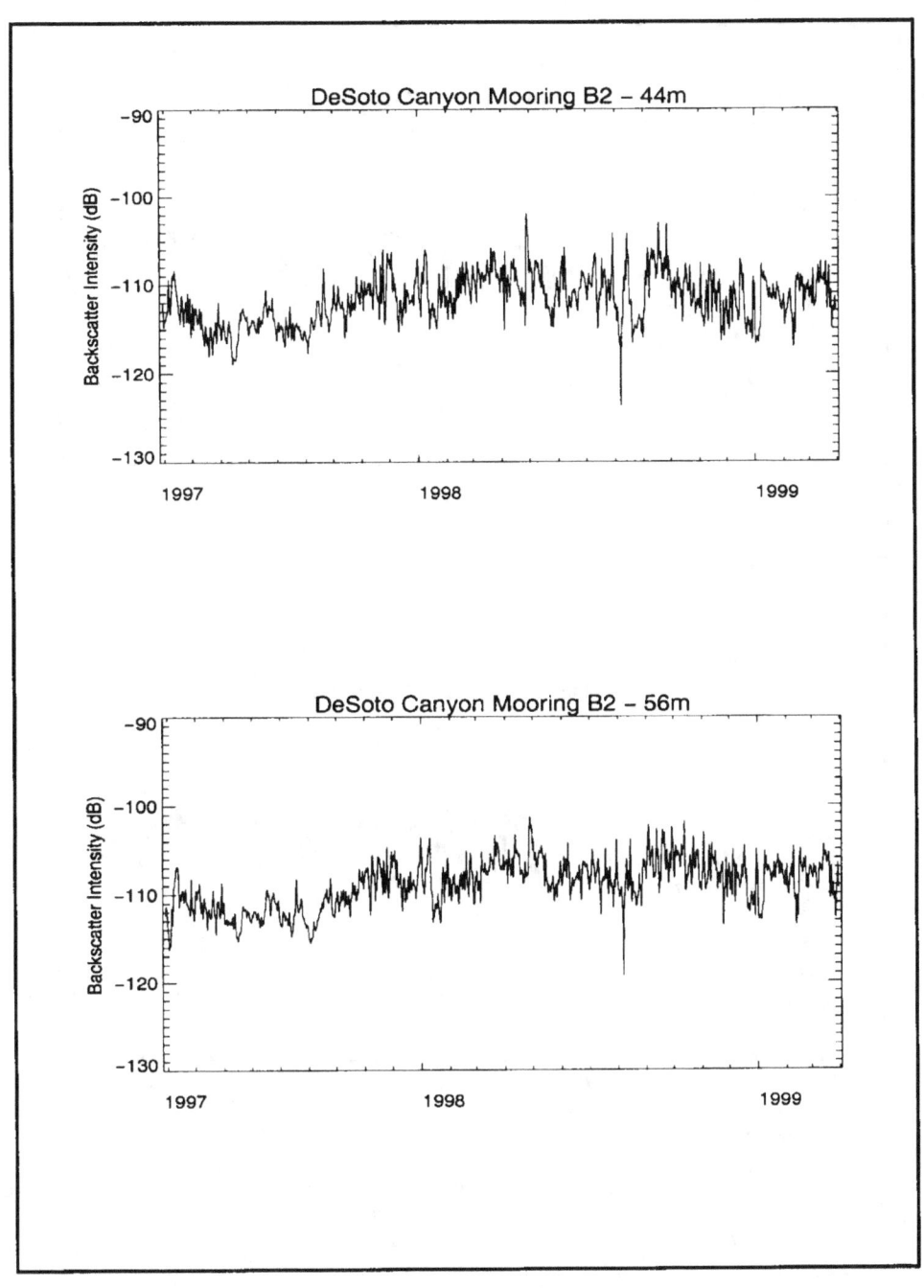

59

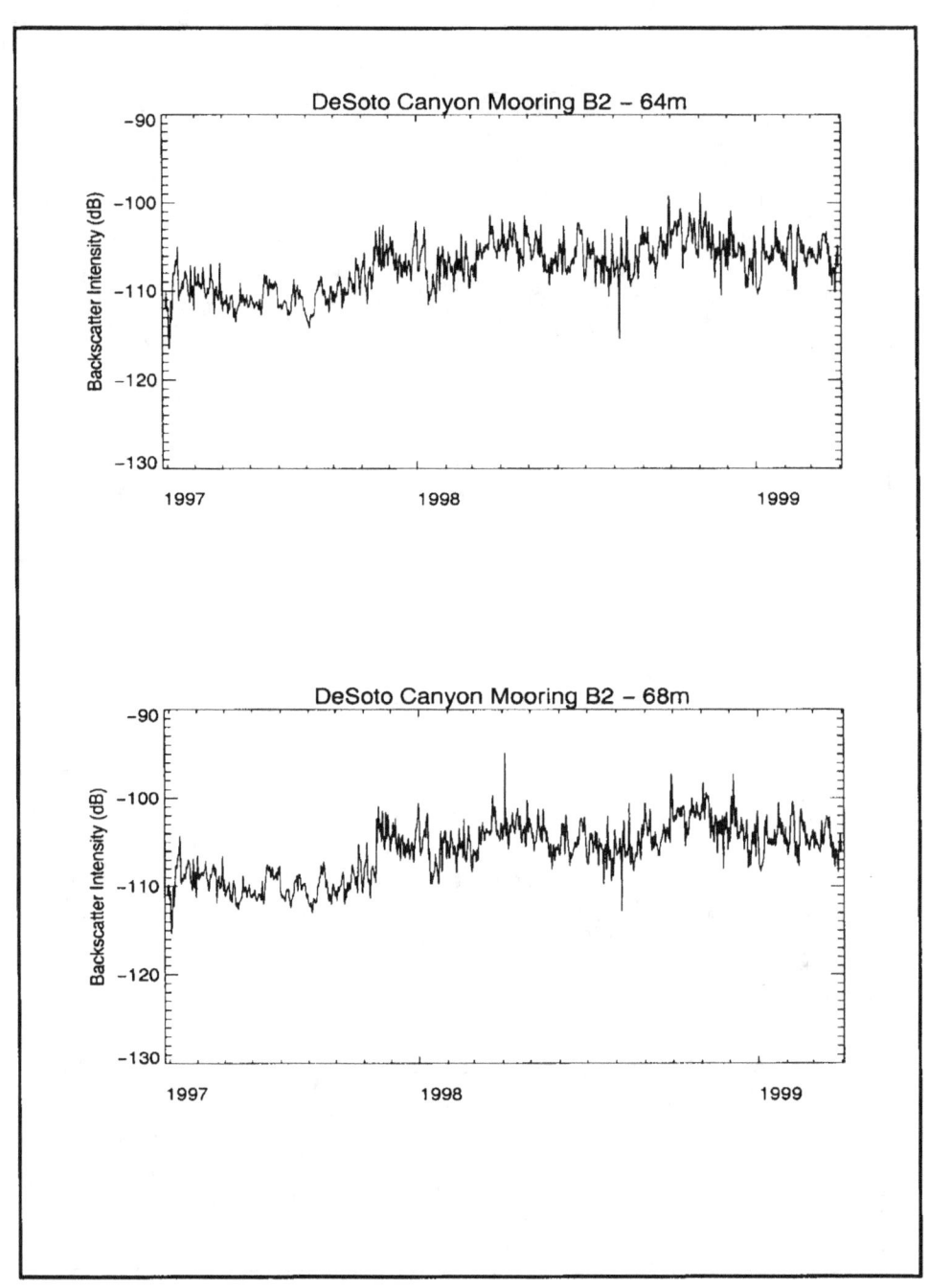

60

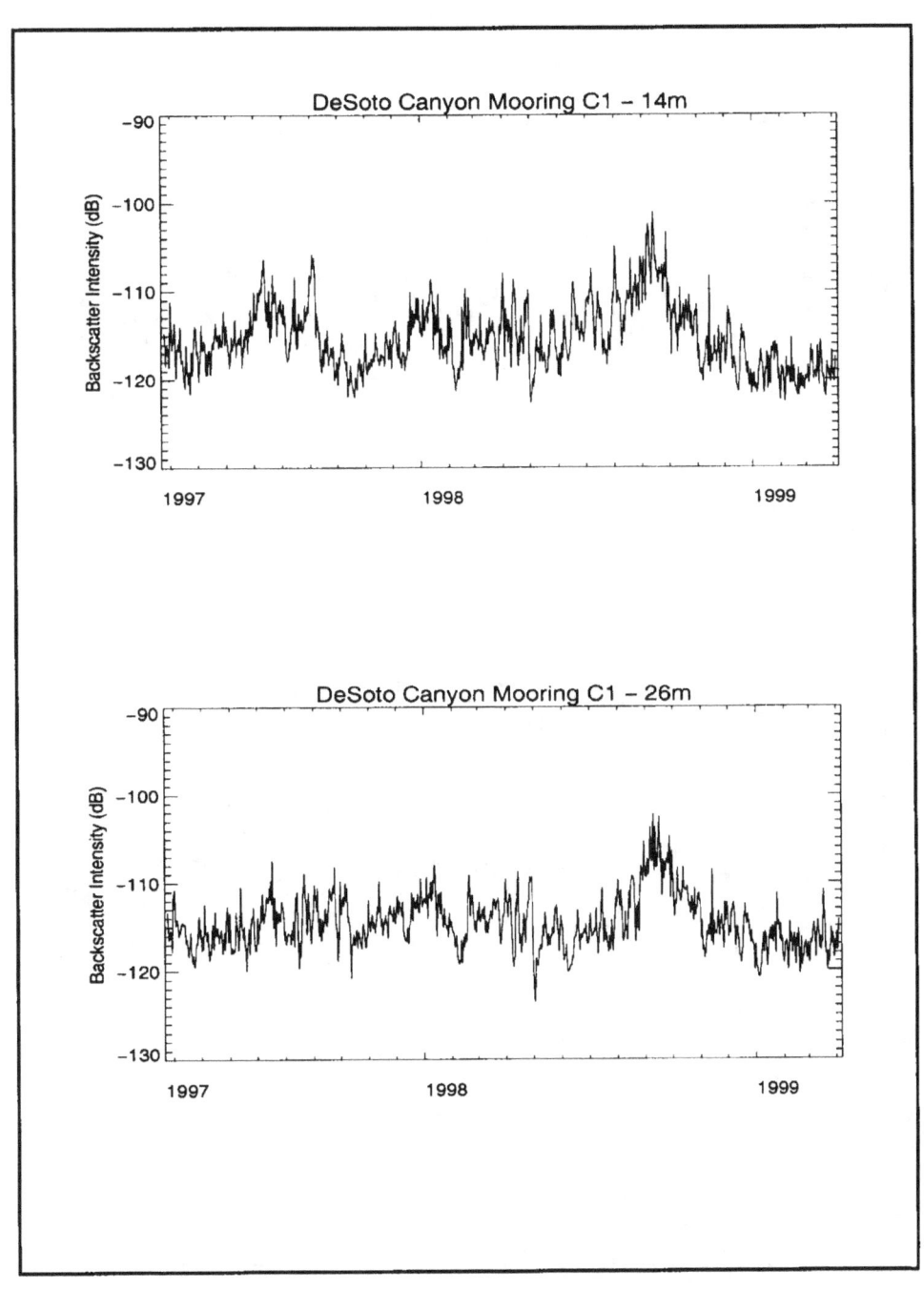

61

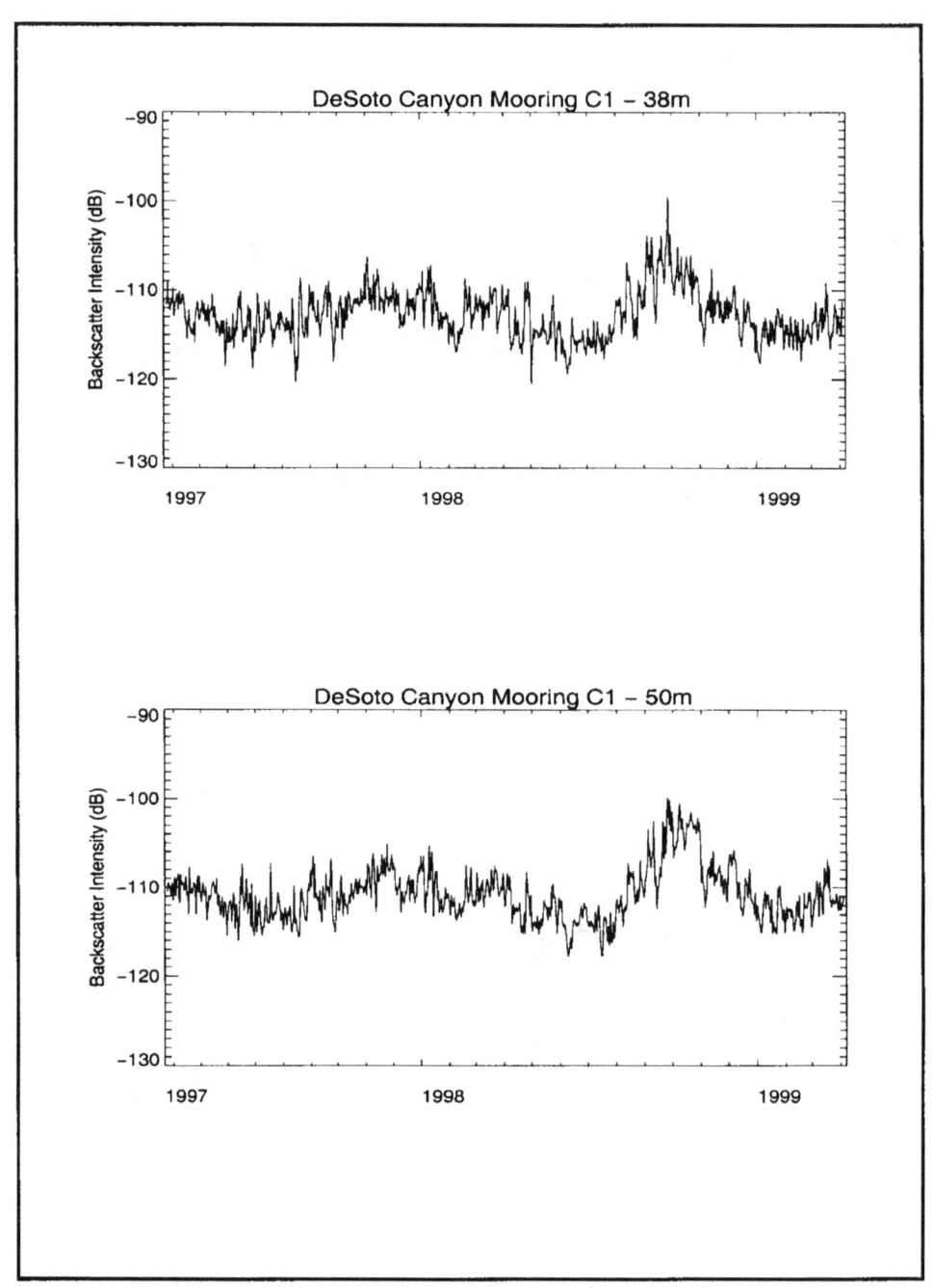

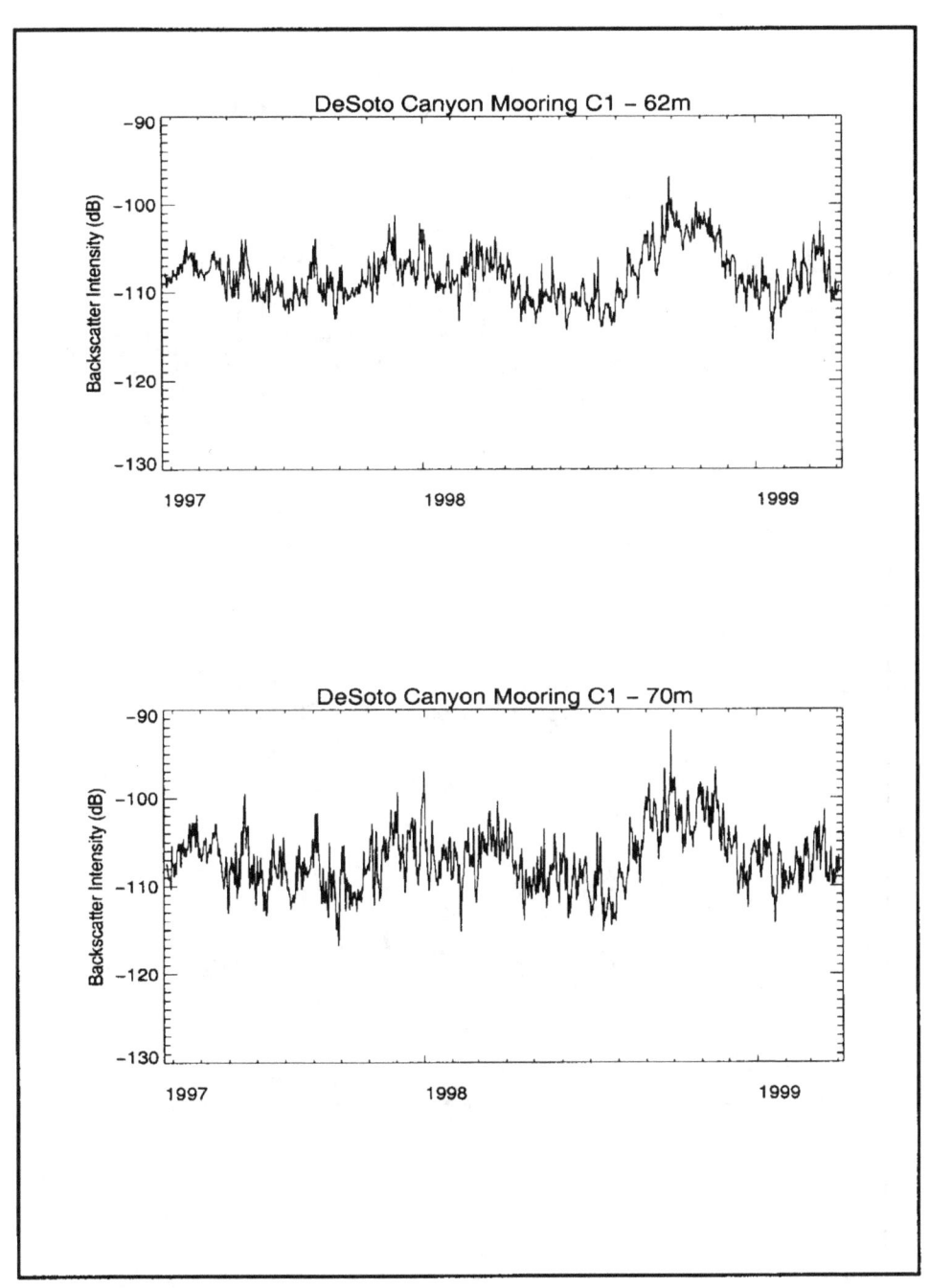

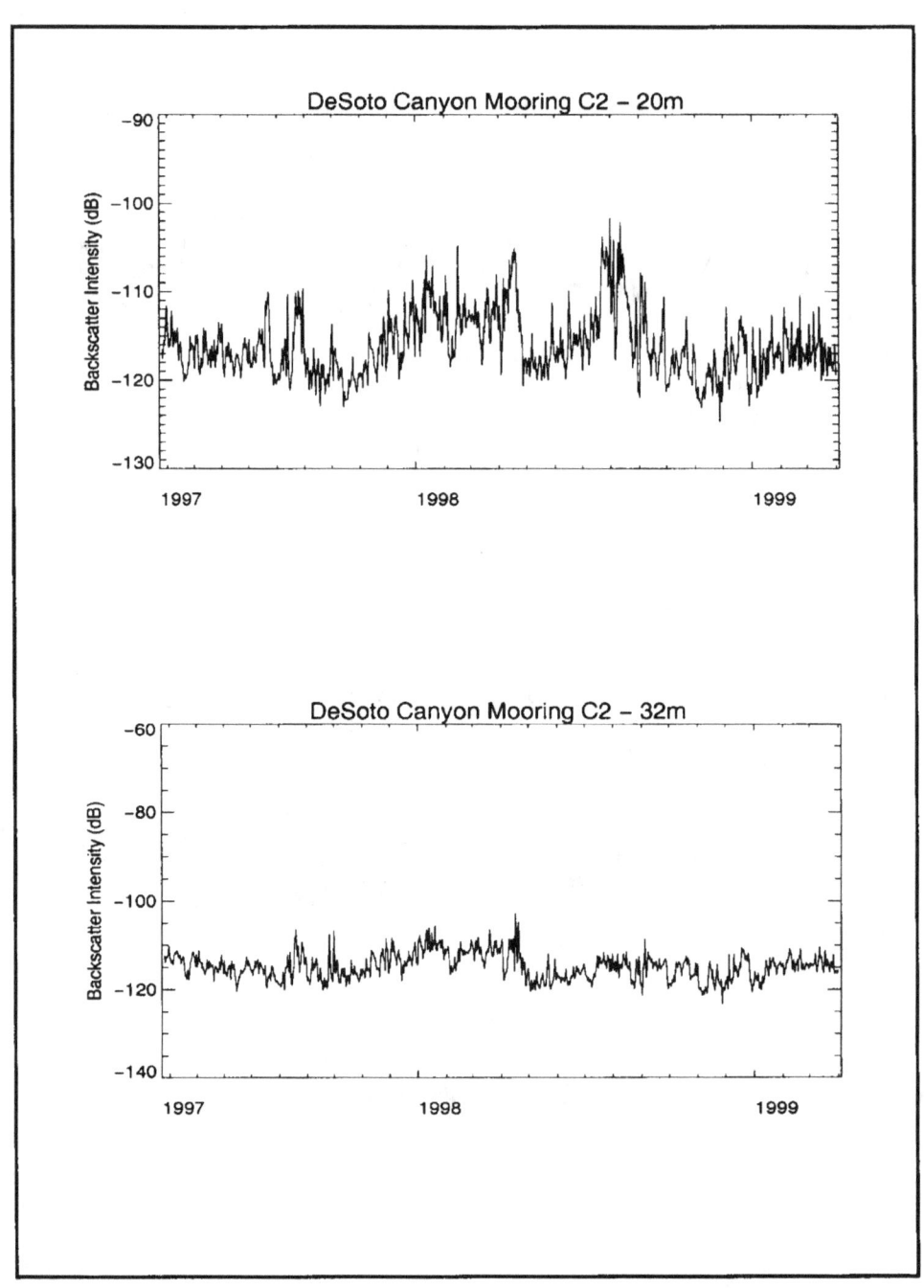

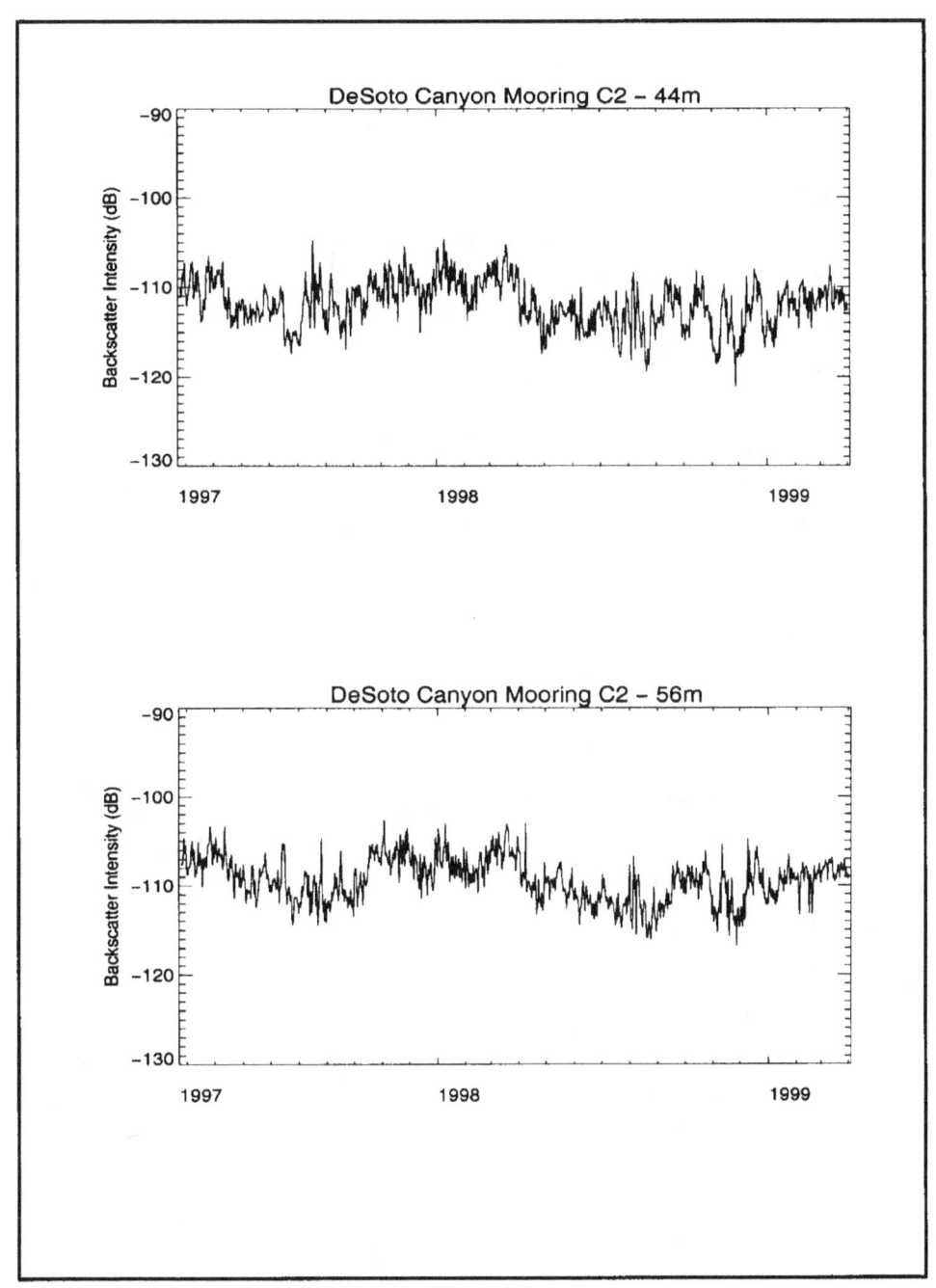

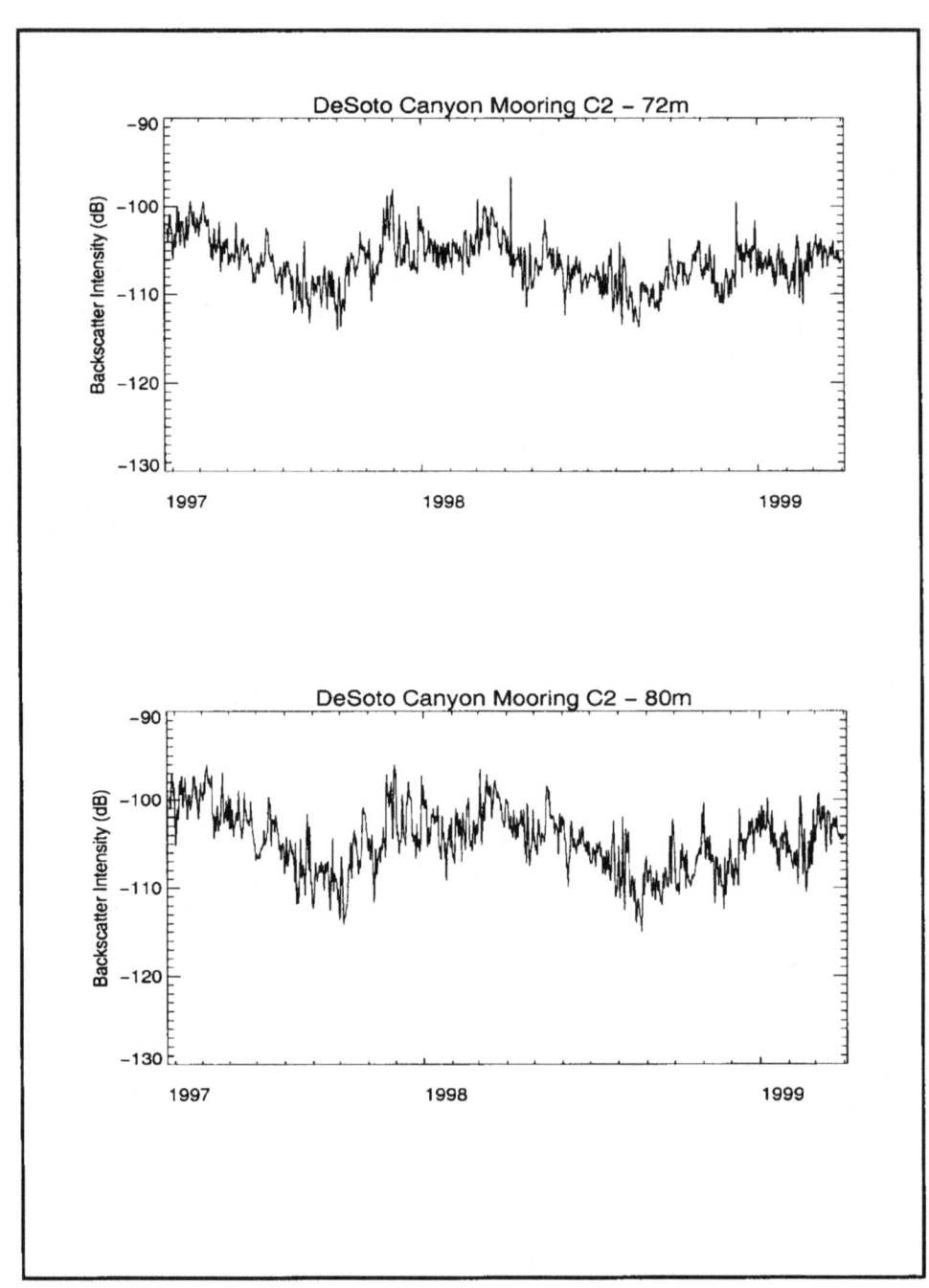

66

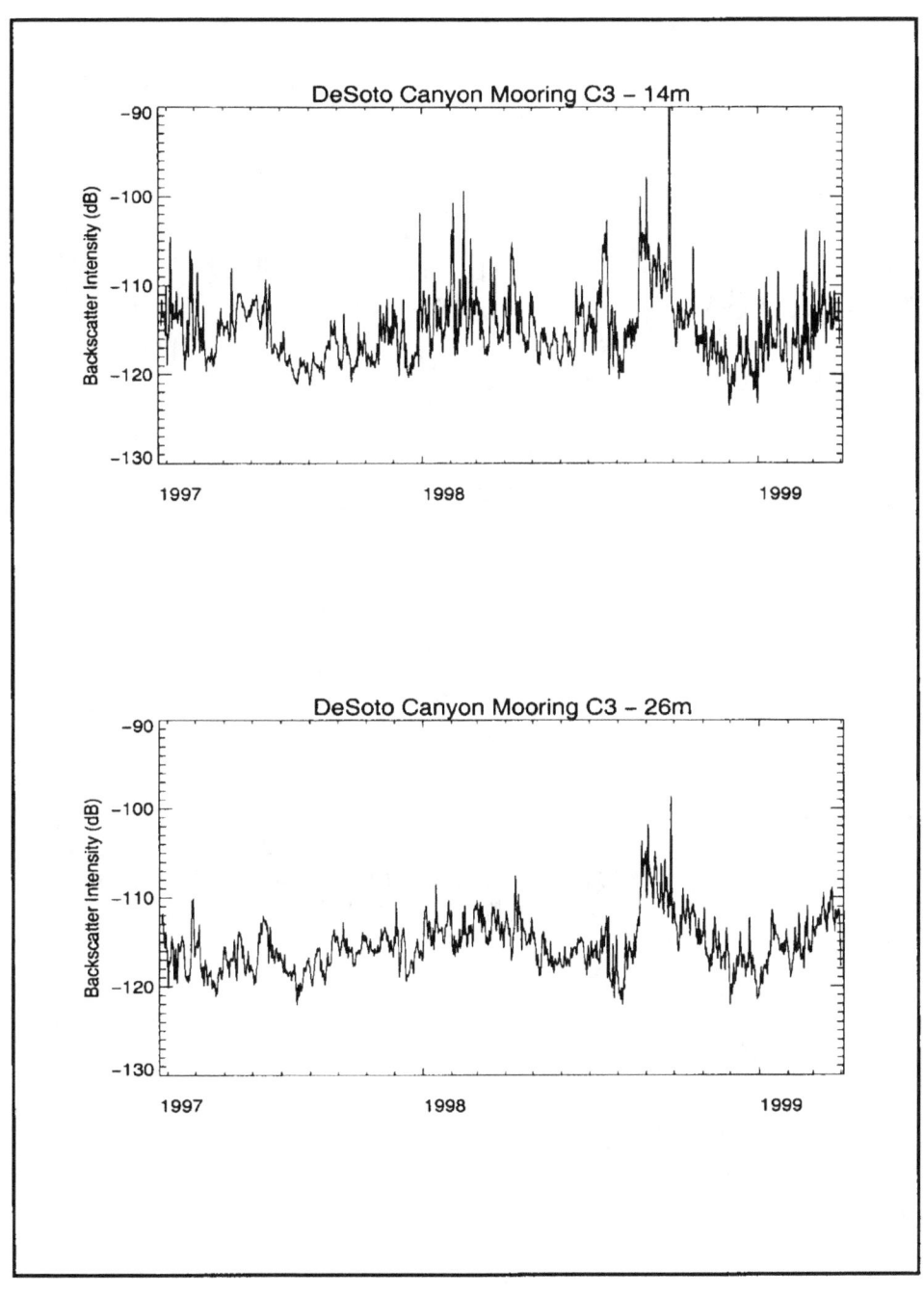

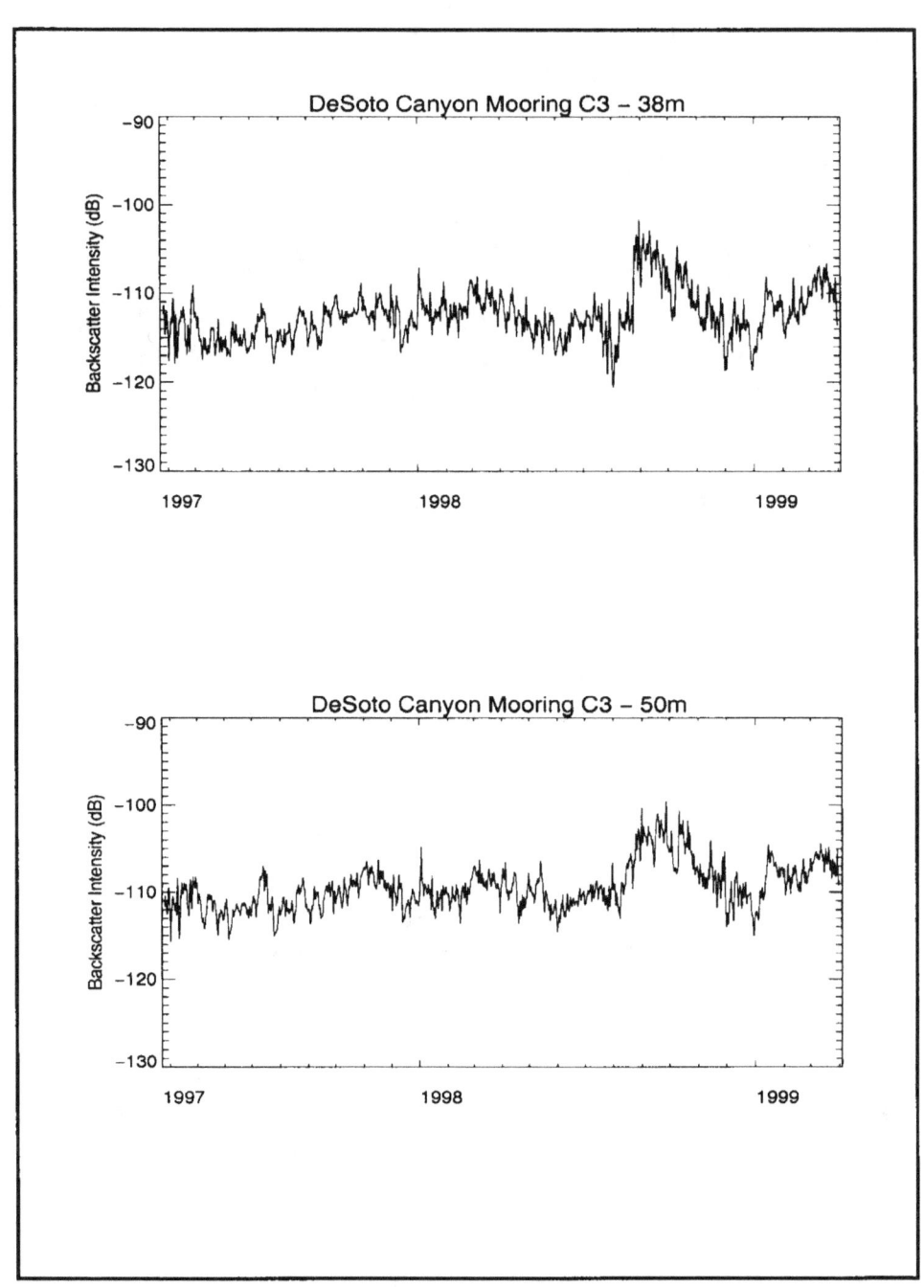

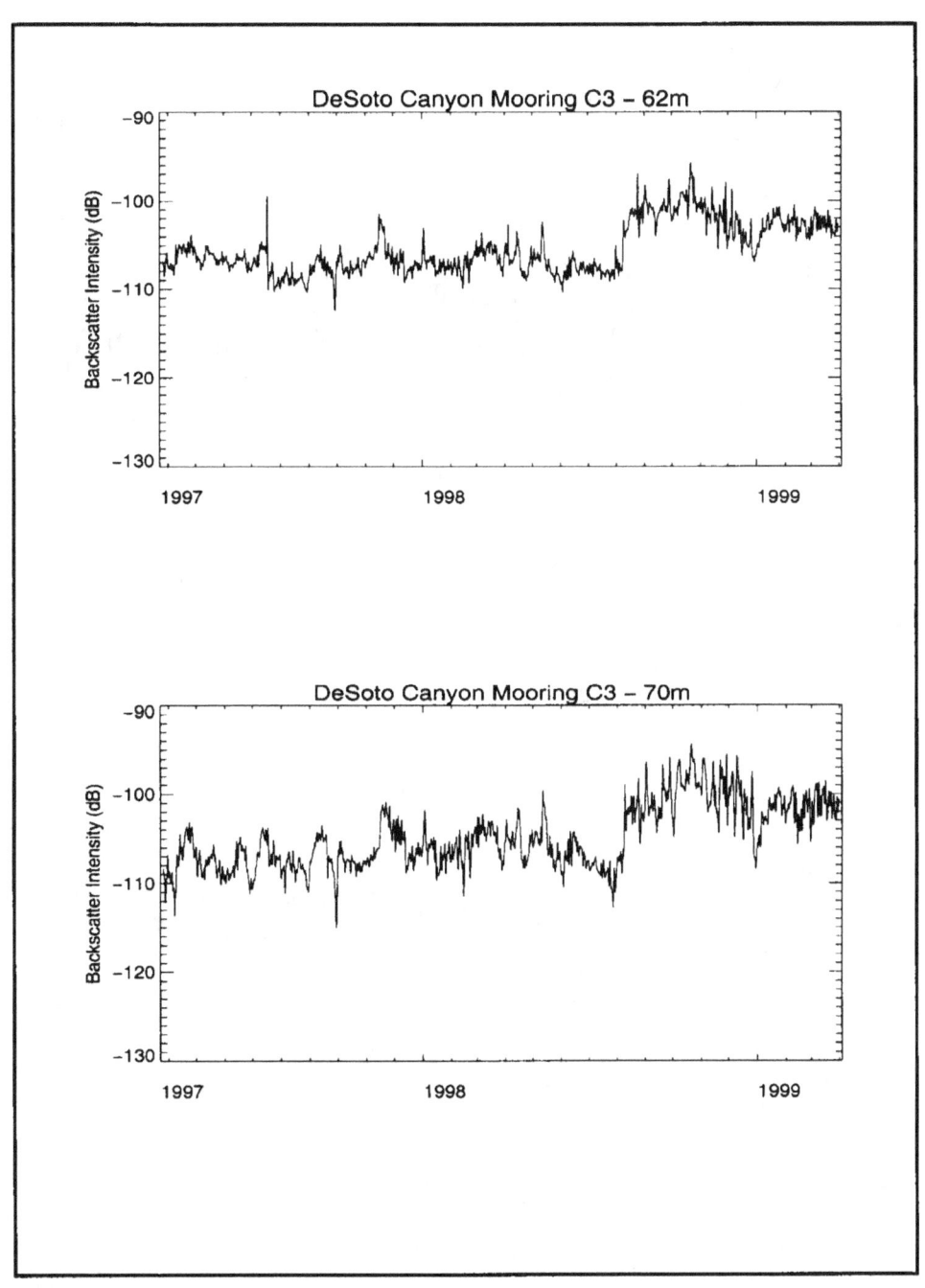

69

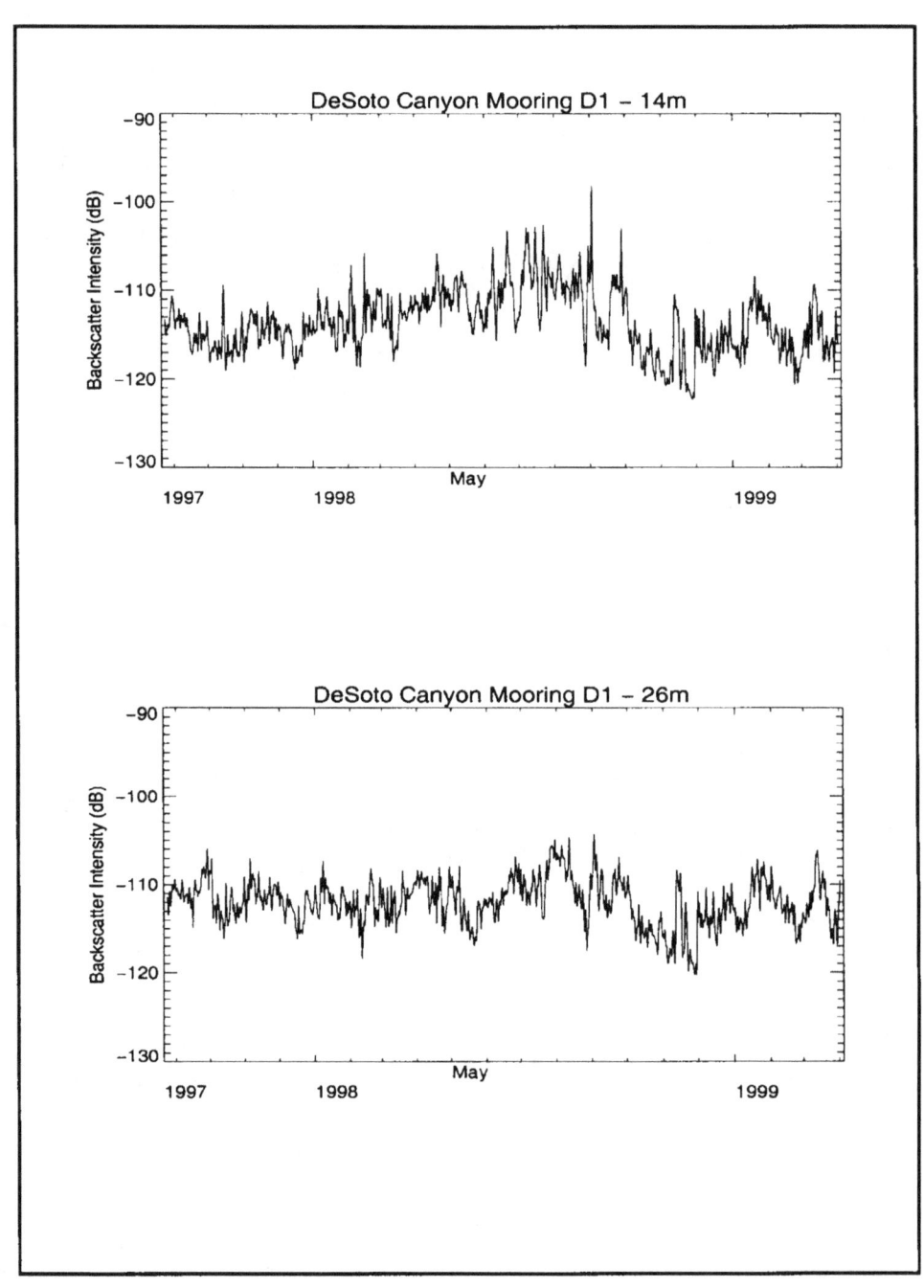

70

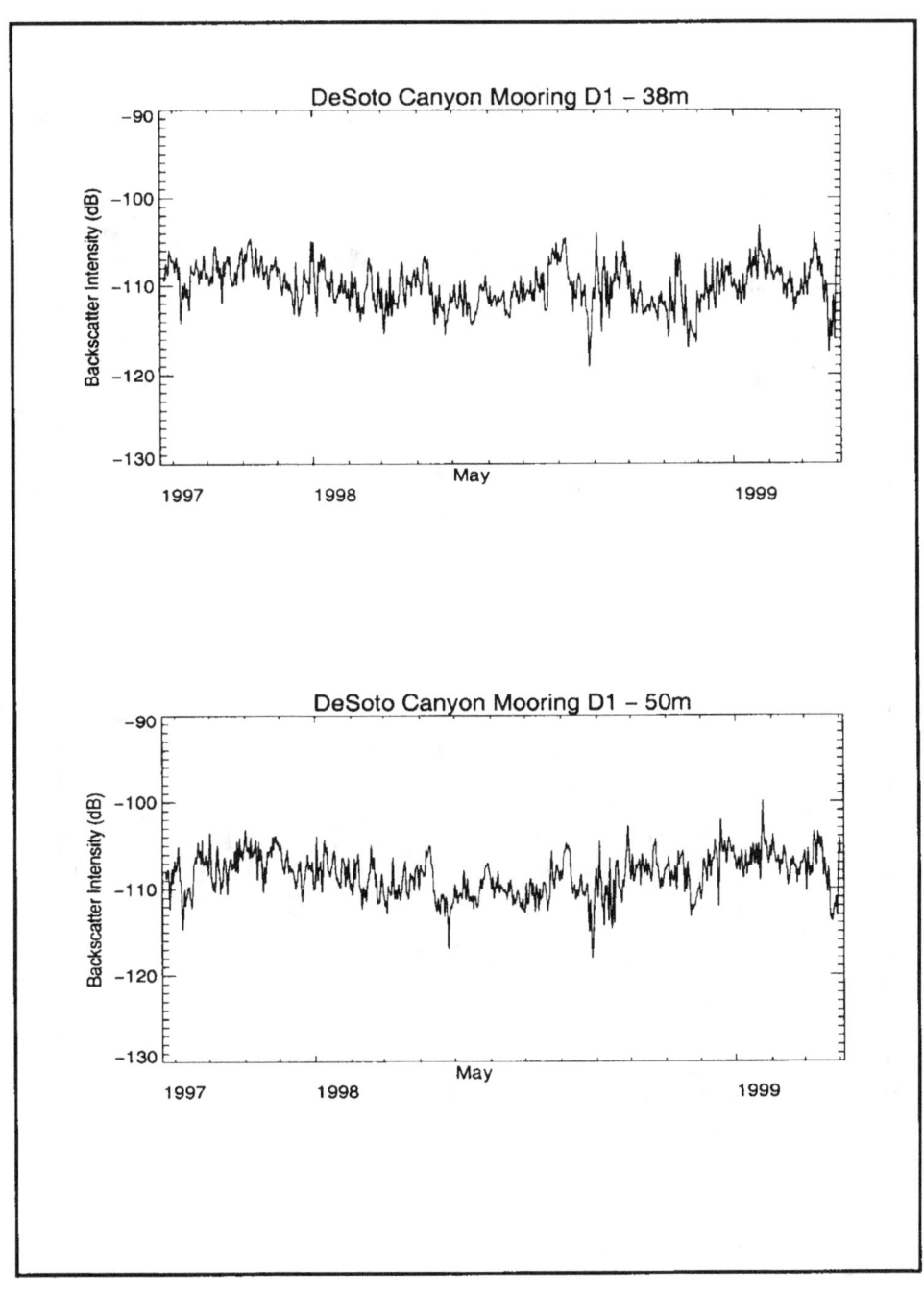

71

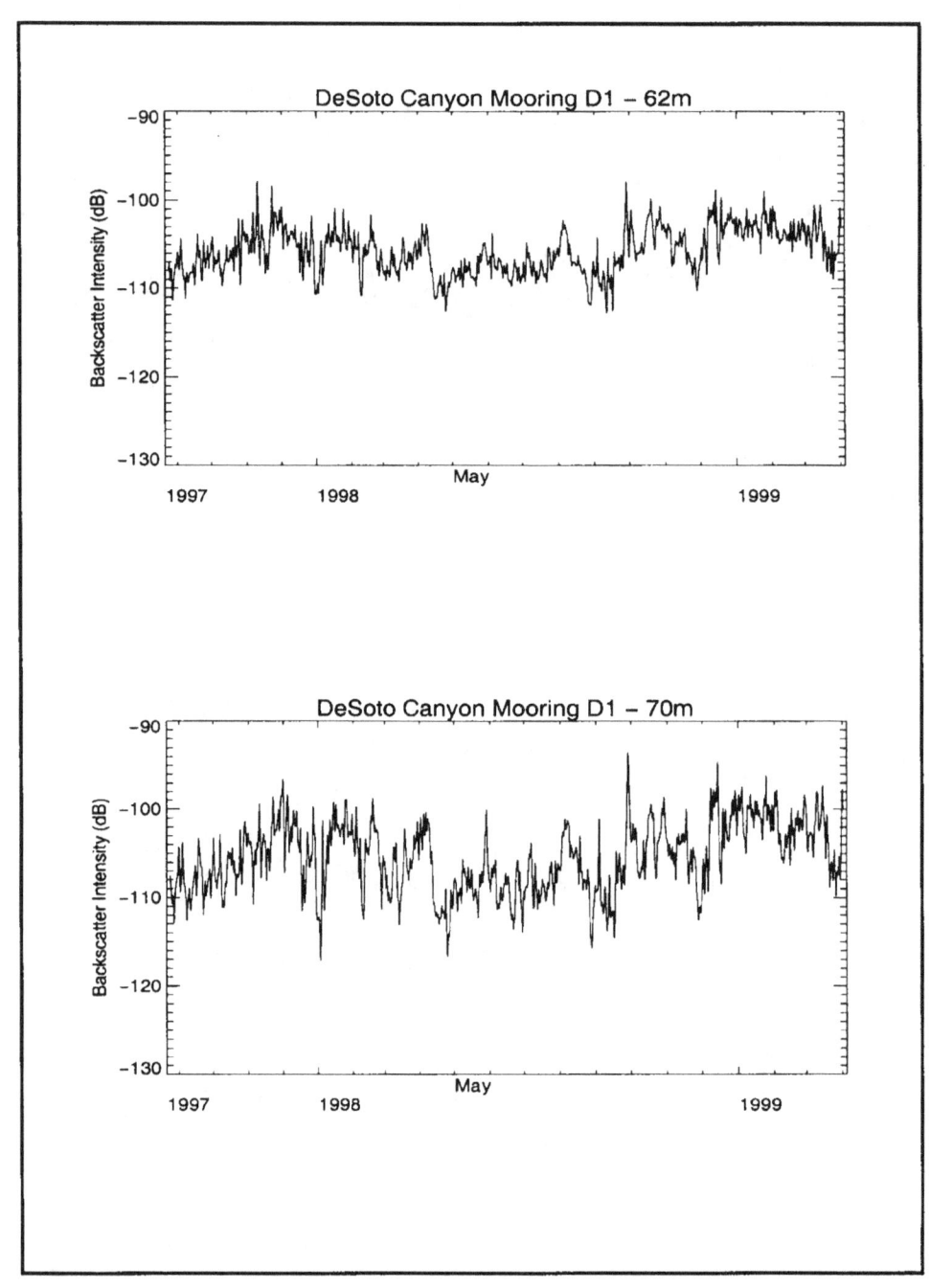

72

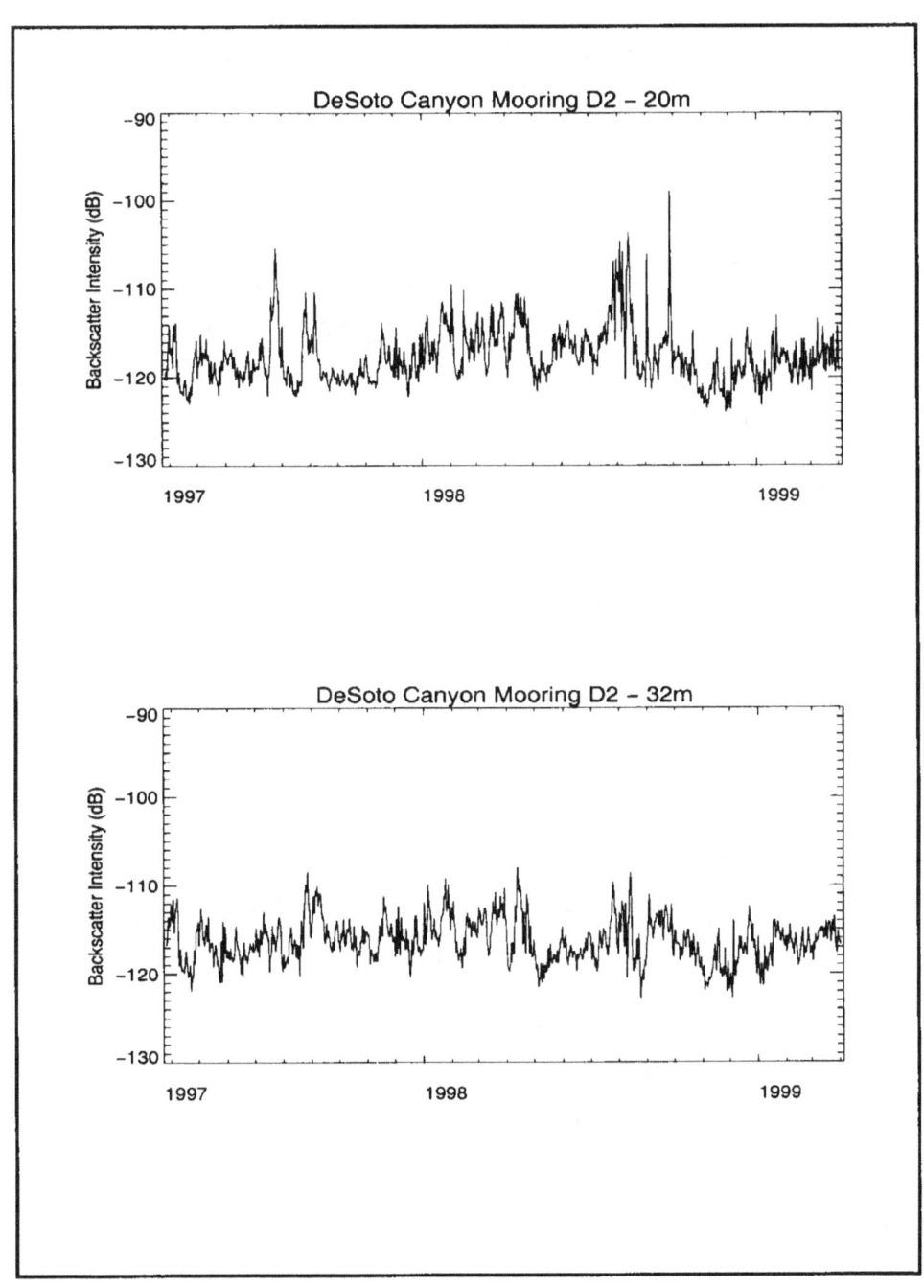

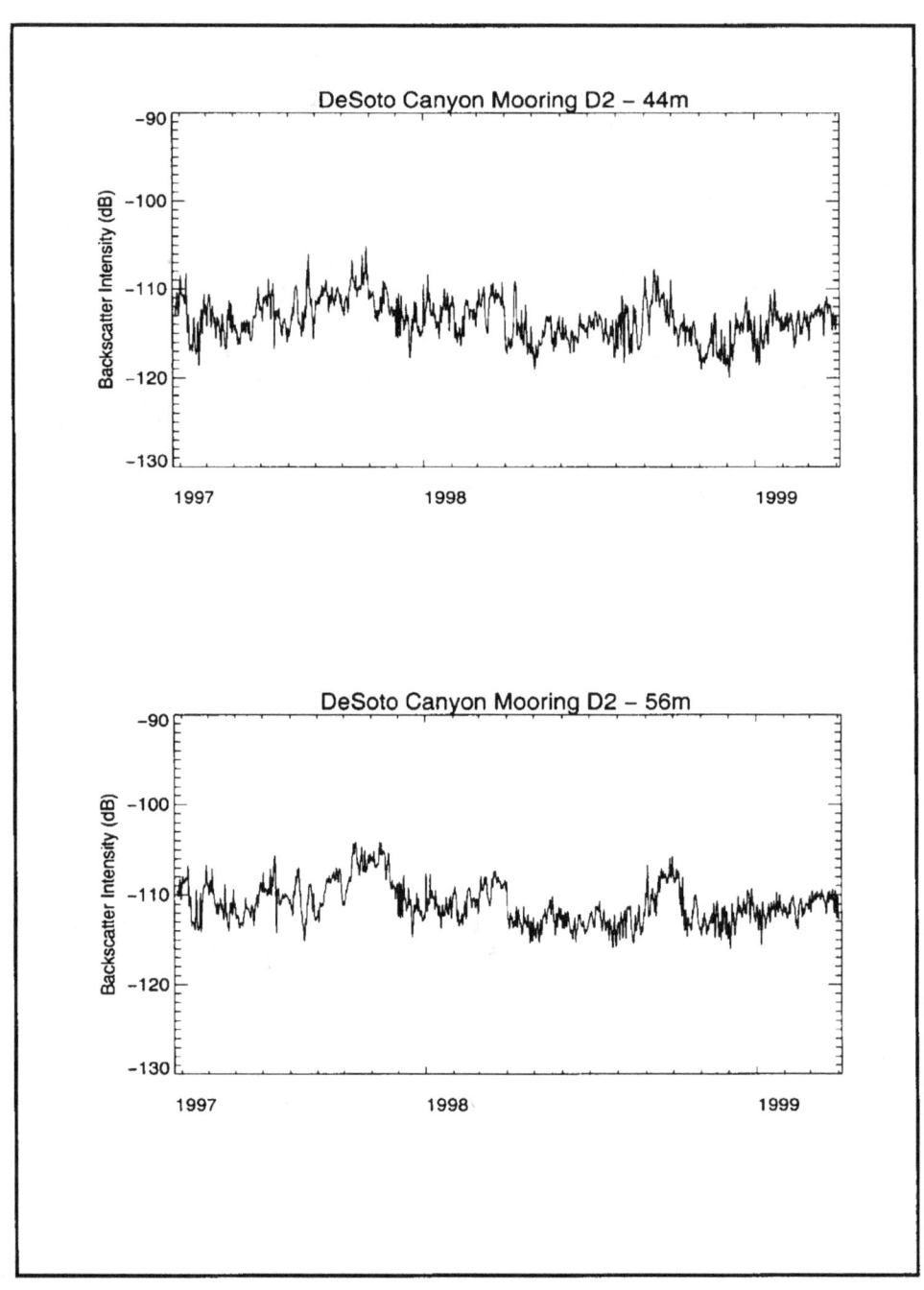

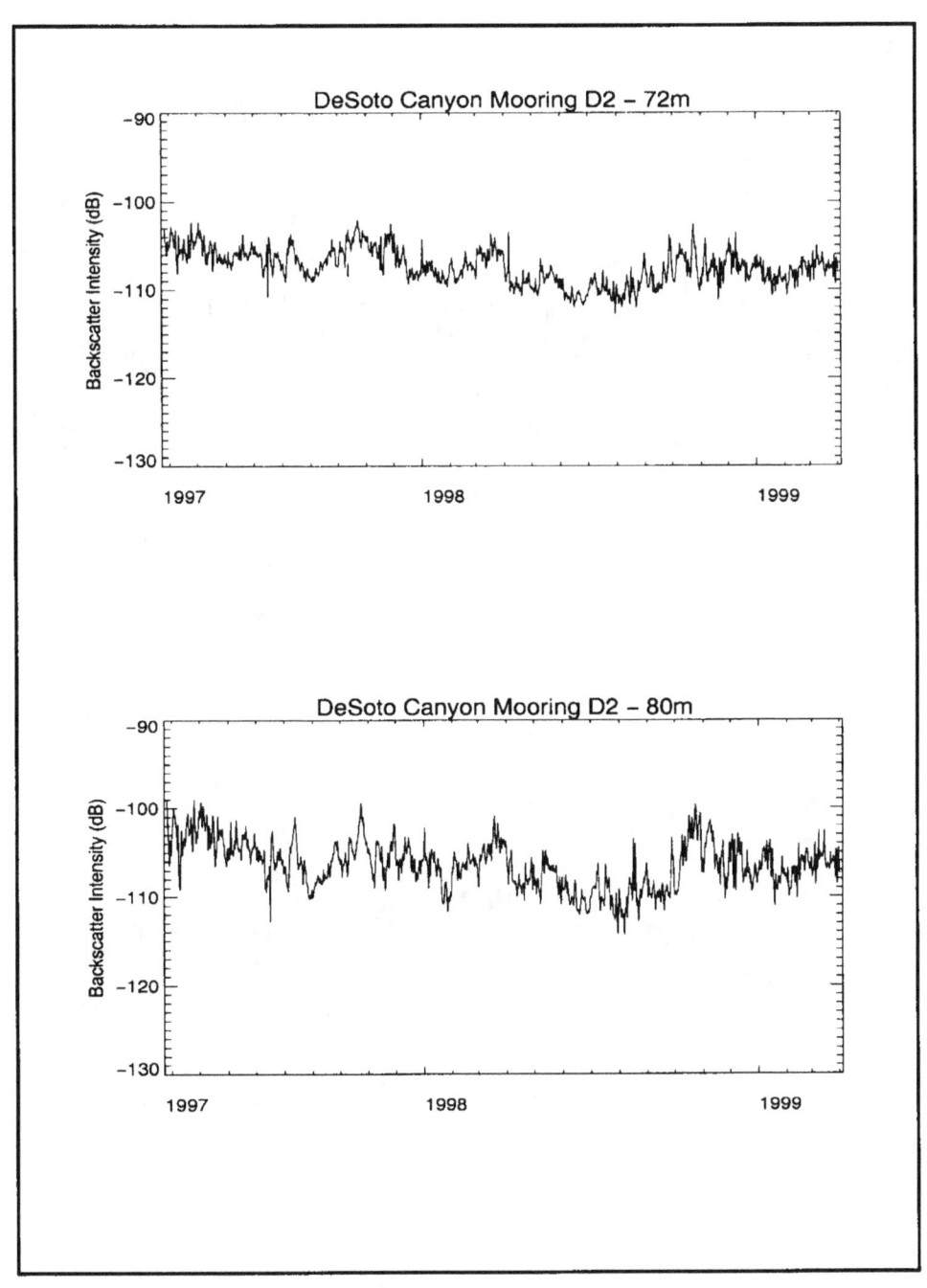

75

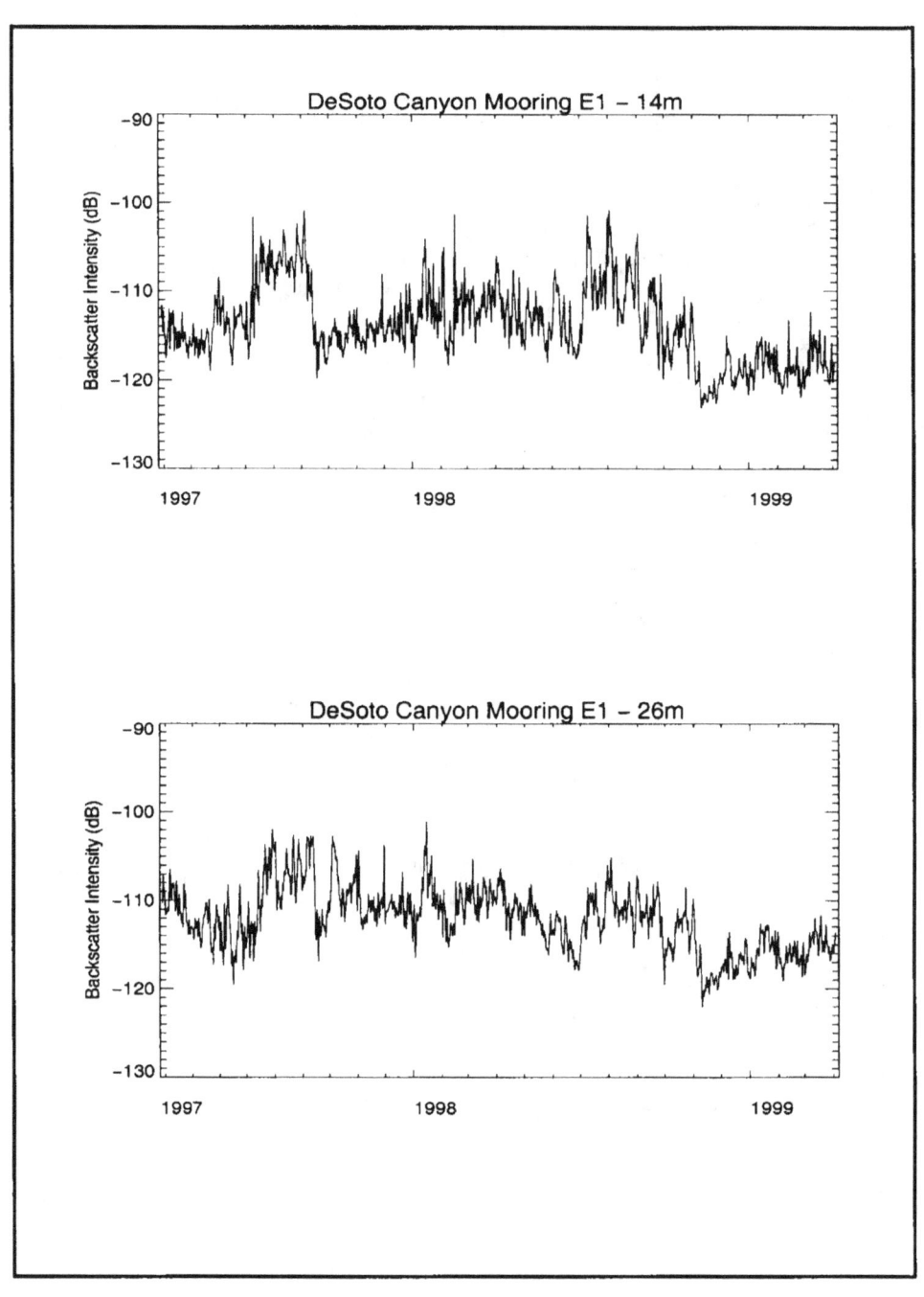

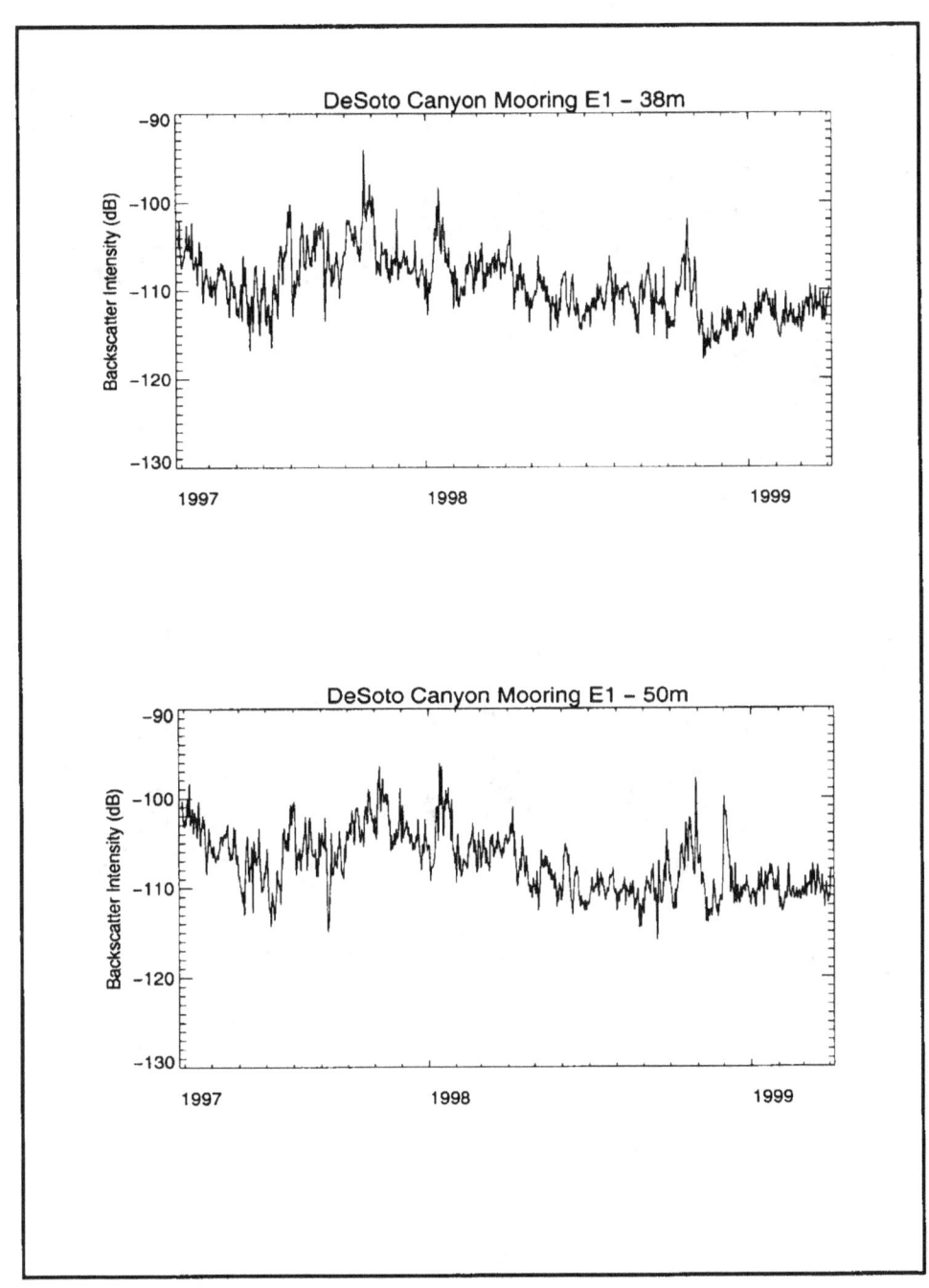

77

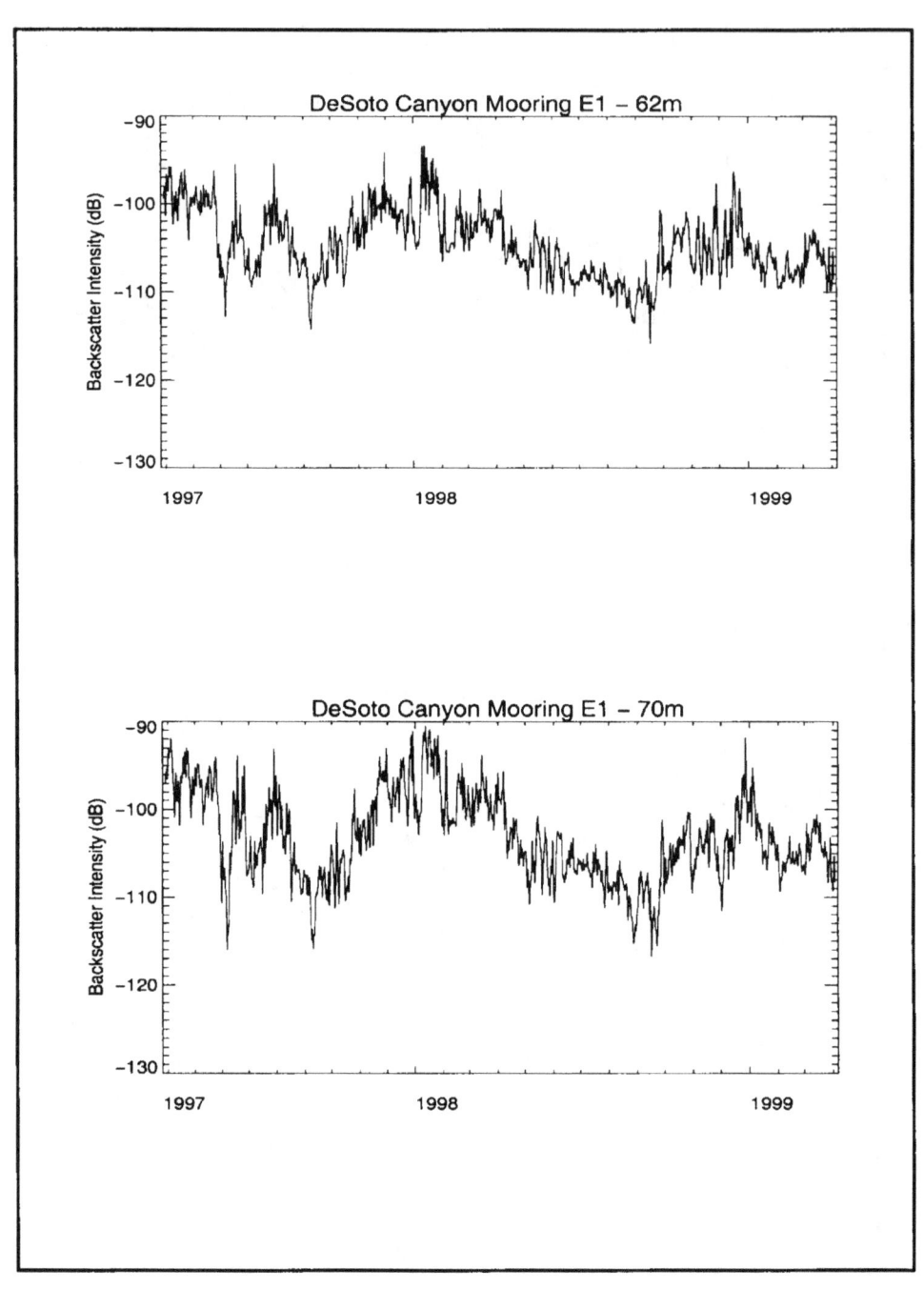

78

APPENDIX B:

**Spectra of 40-hour low-pass filtered acoustic backscatter intensity.
The two records per panel present spectra for the pairs of depths featured in Appendix A.**

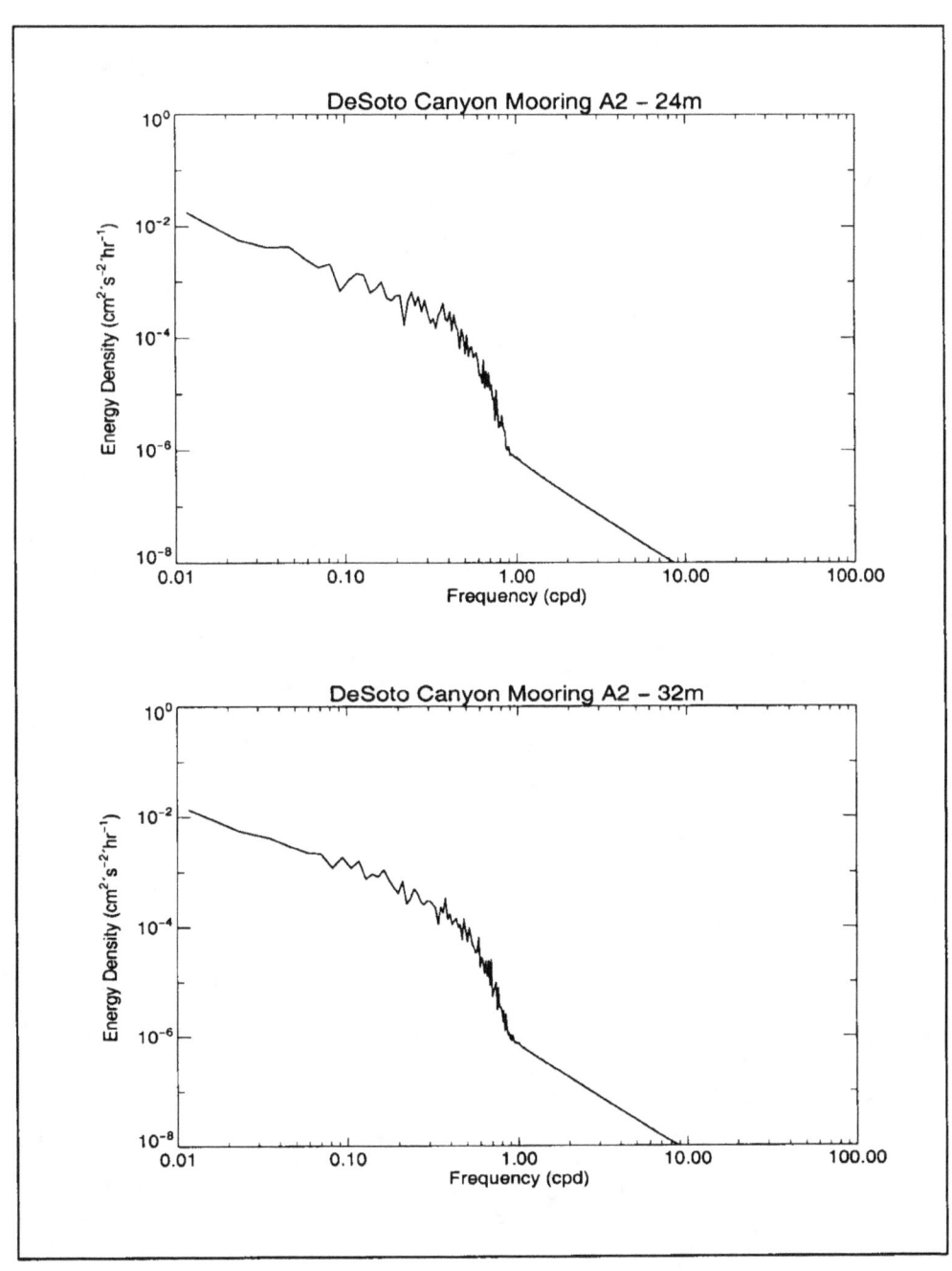

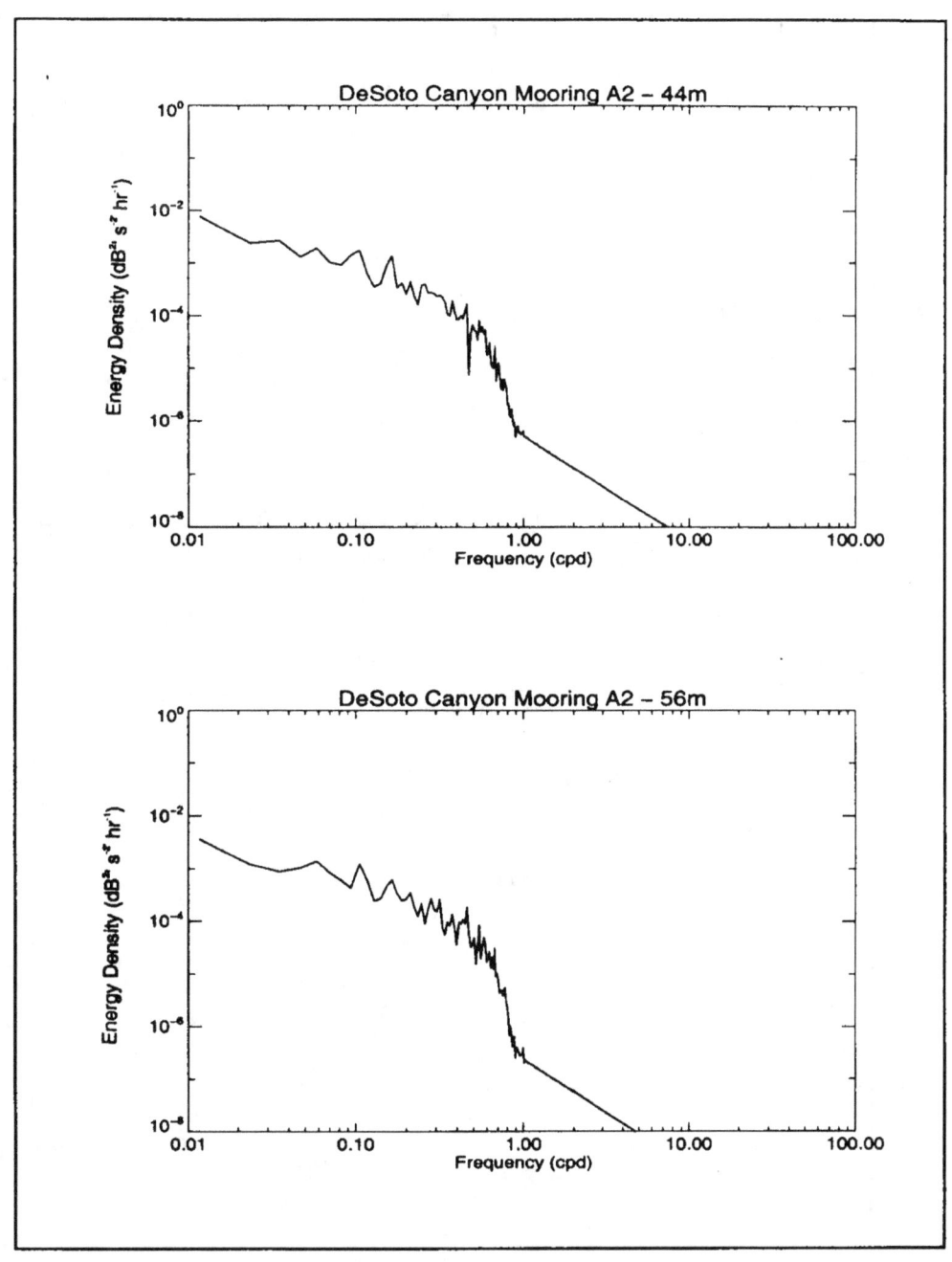

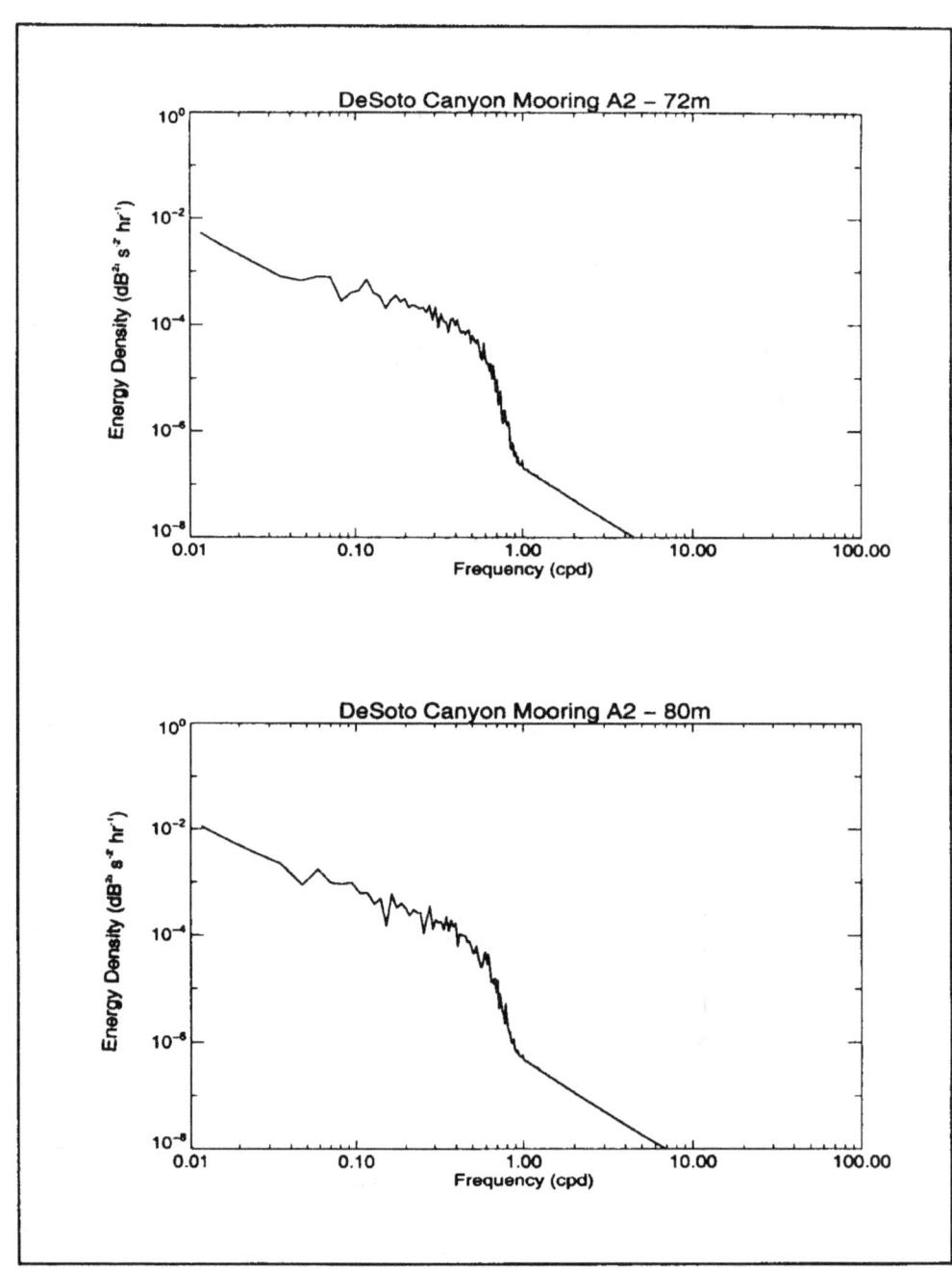

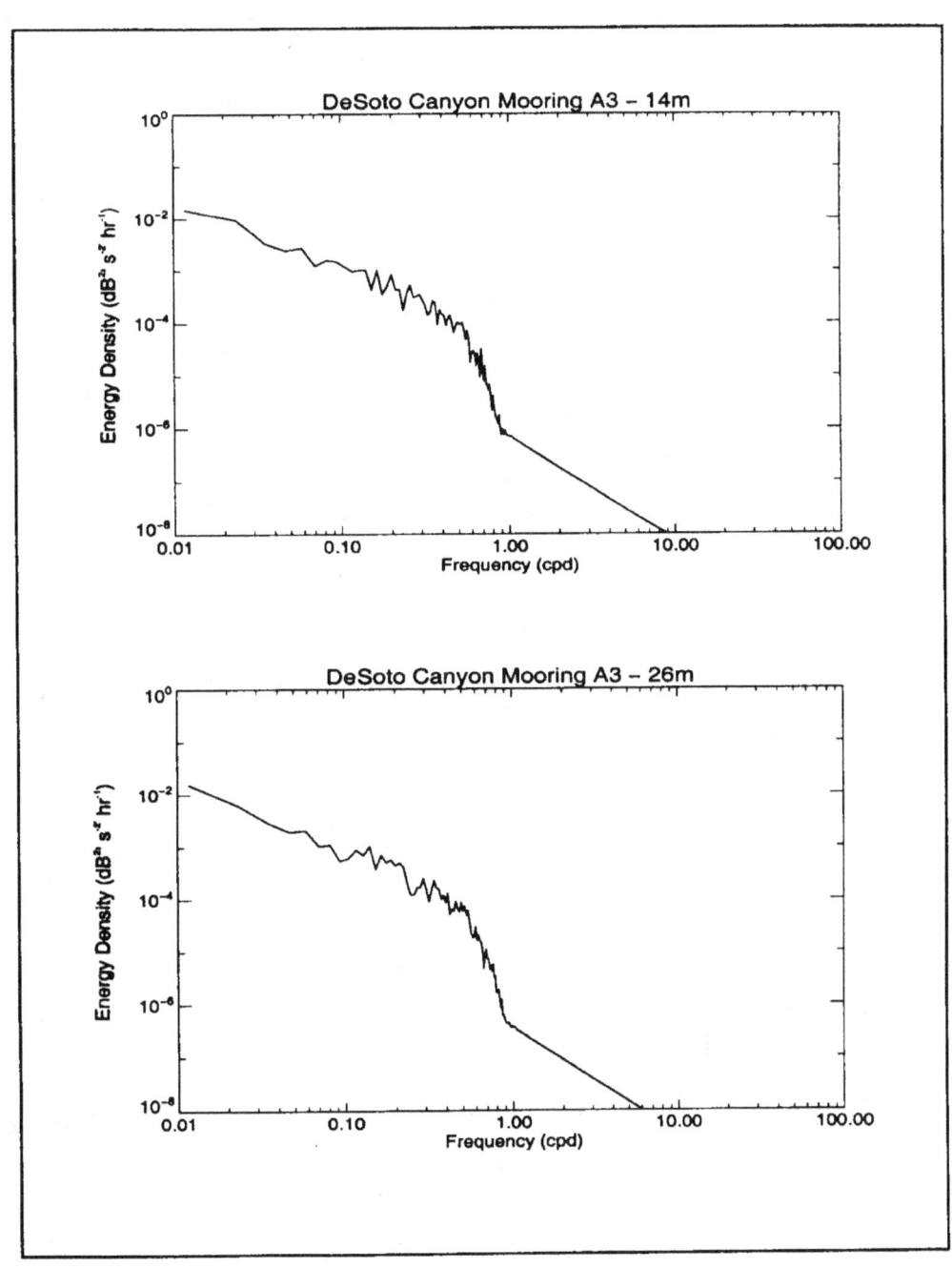

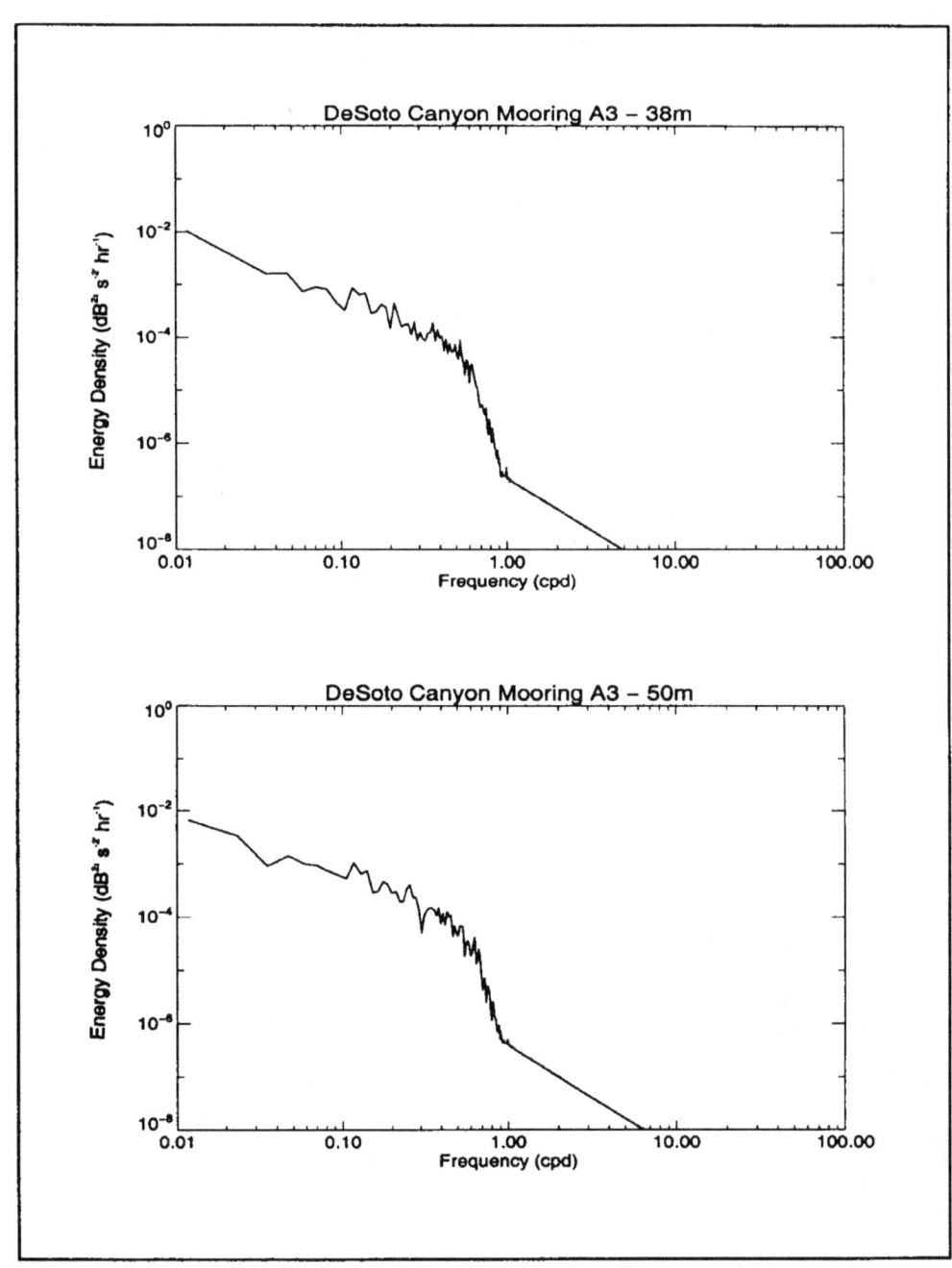

86

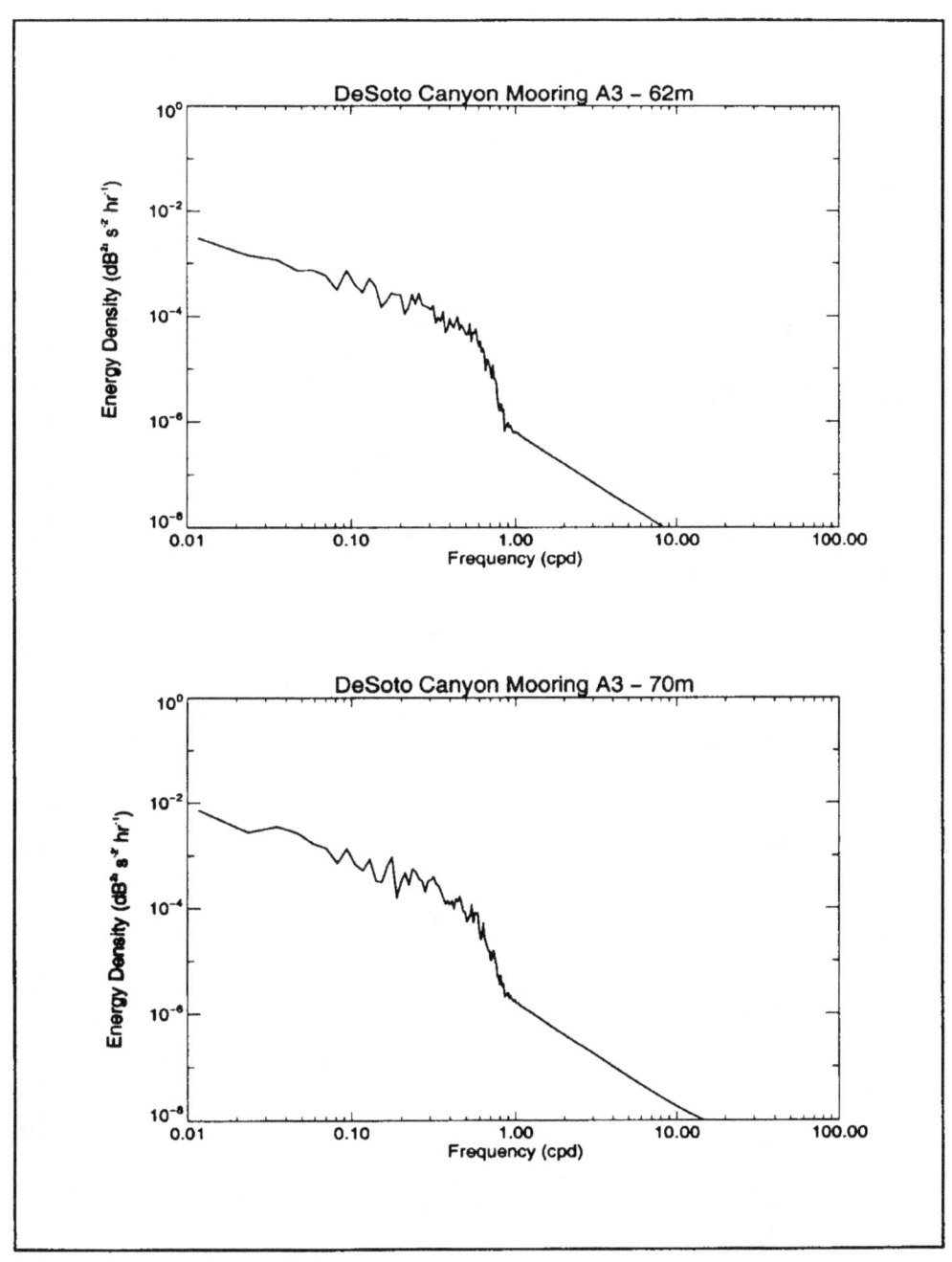

87

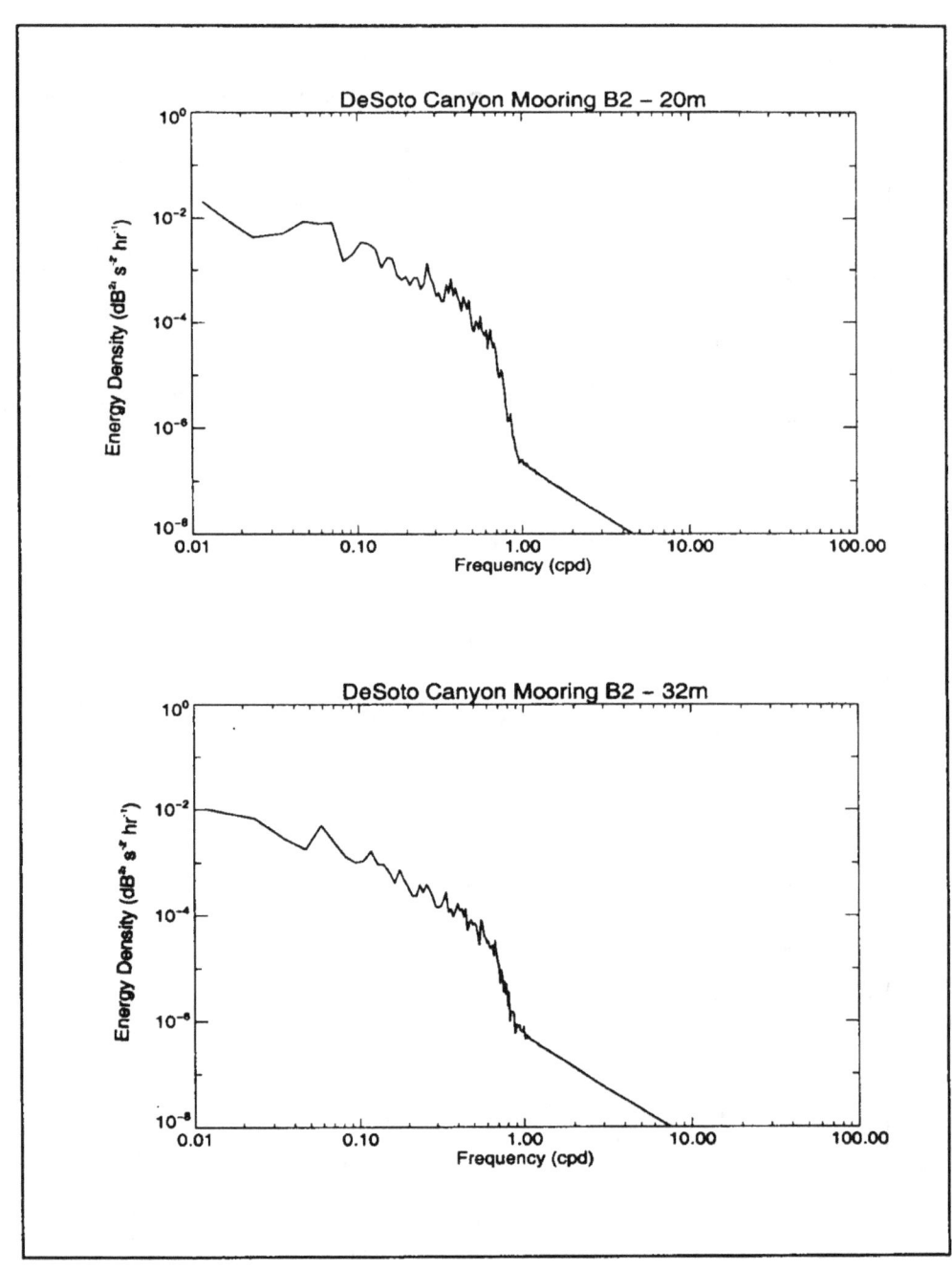

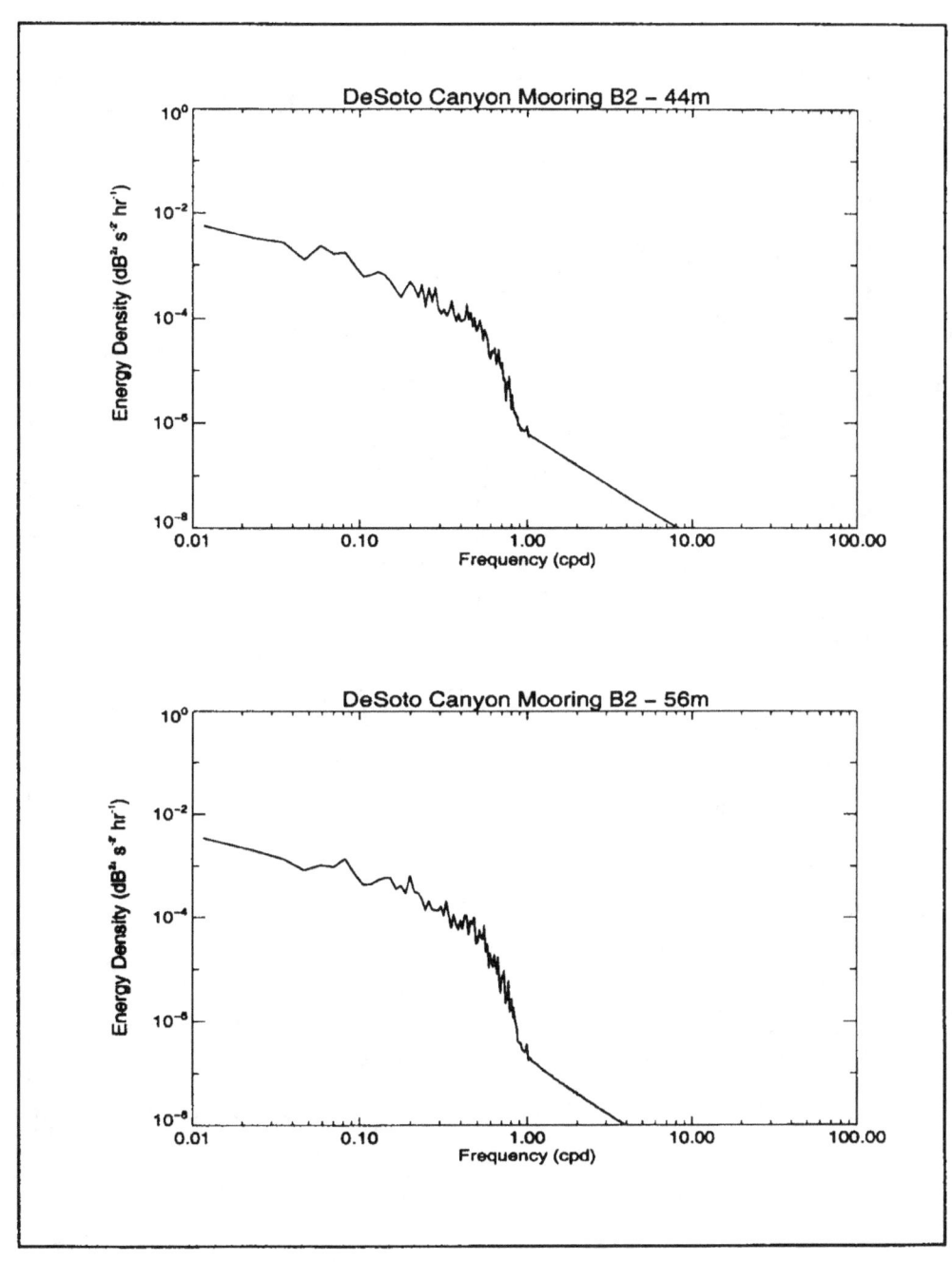

89

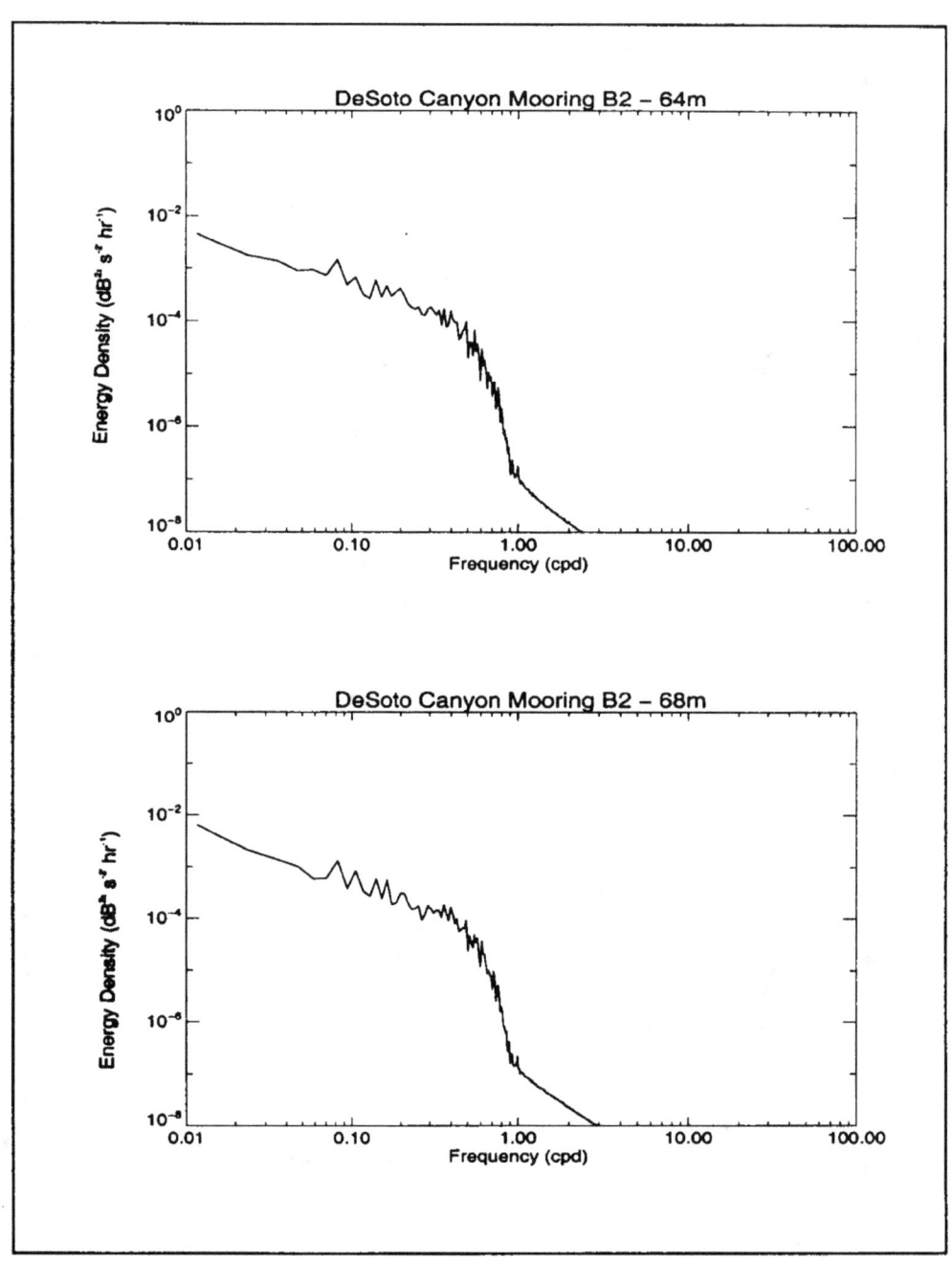

90

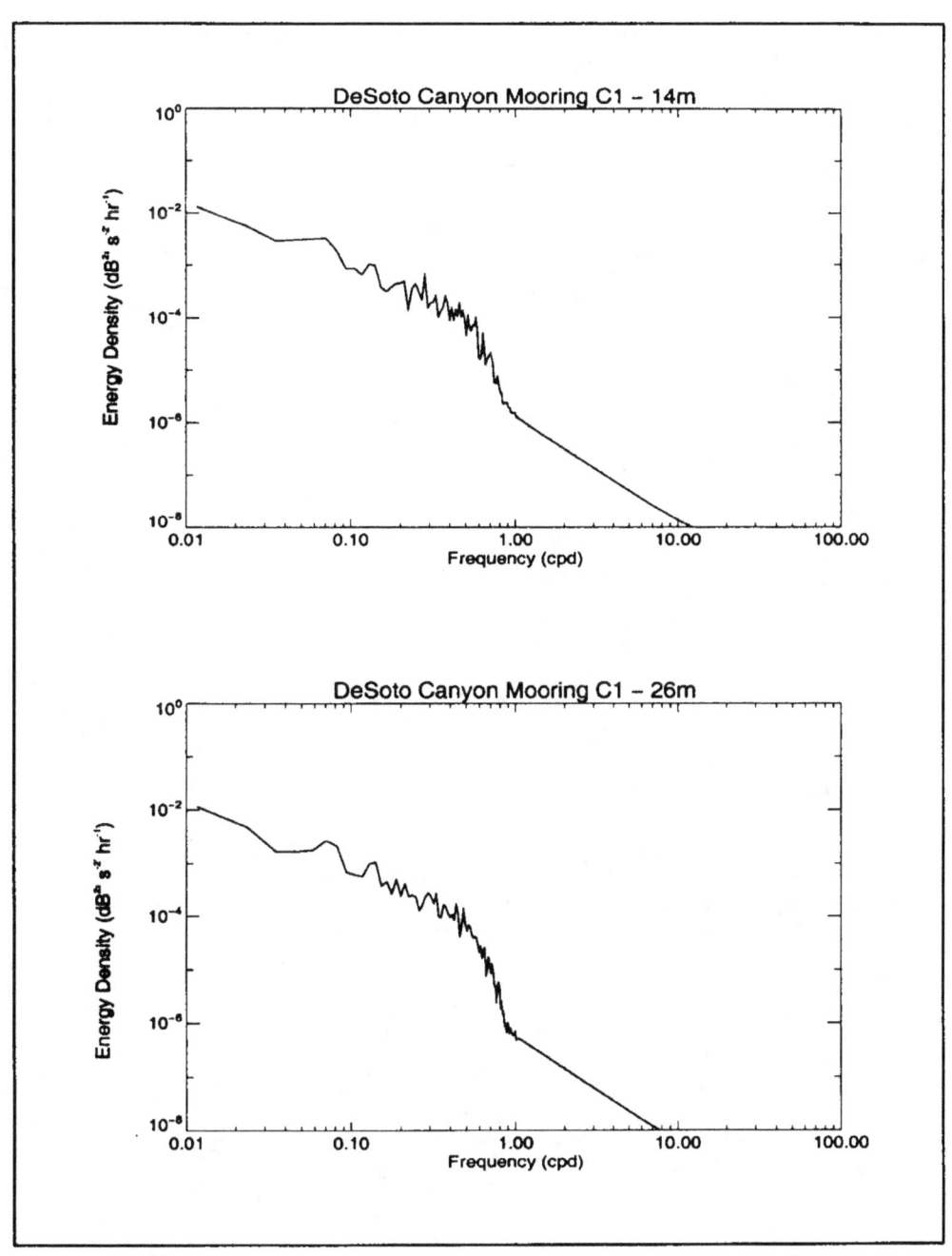

DeSoto Canyon Mooring C1 – 14m

DeSoto Canyon Mooring C1 – 26m

91

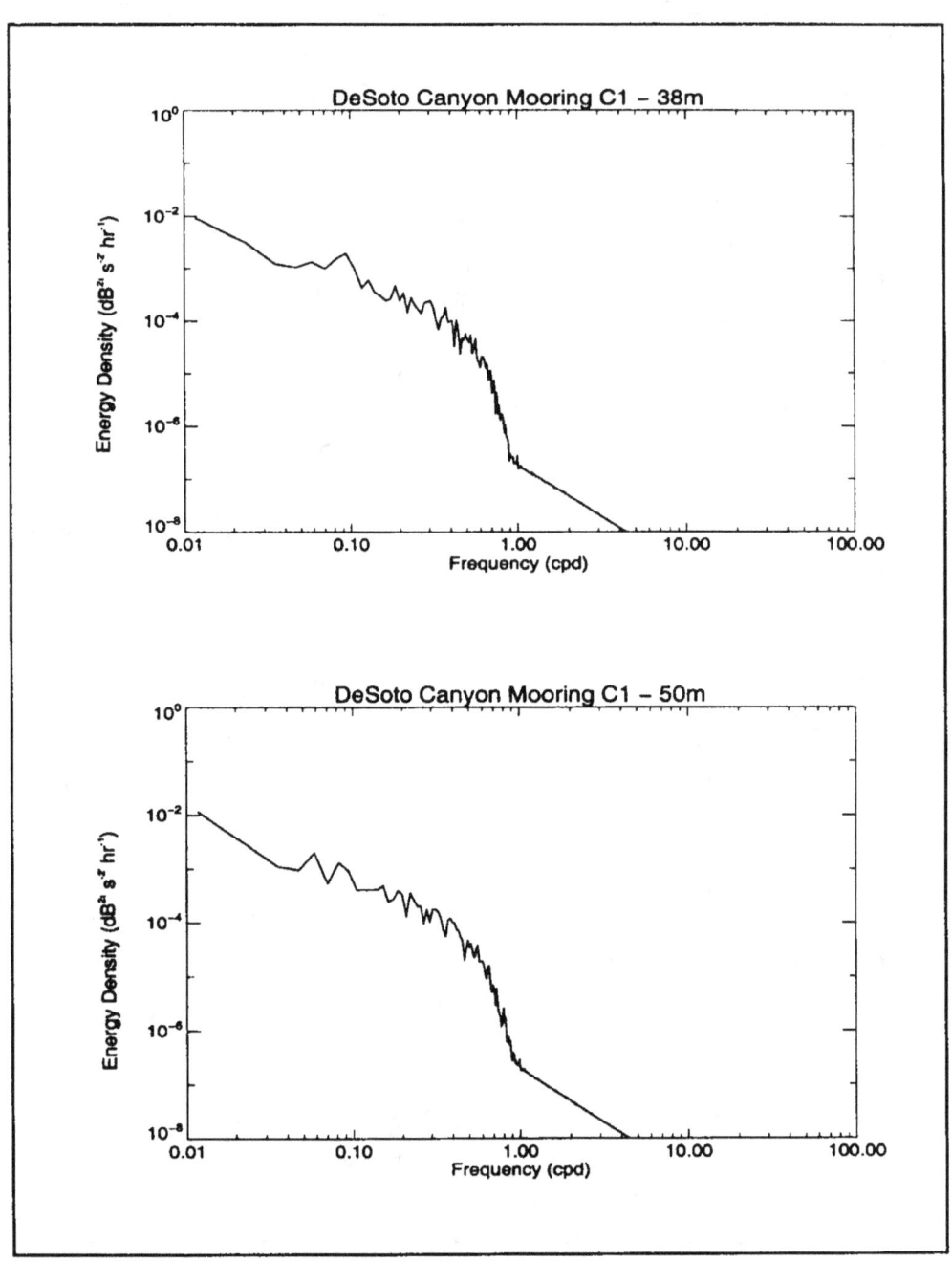

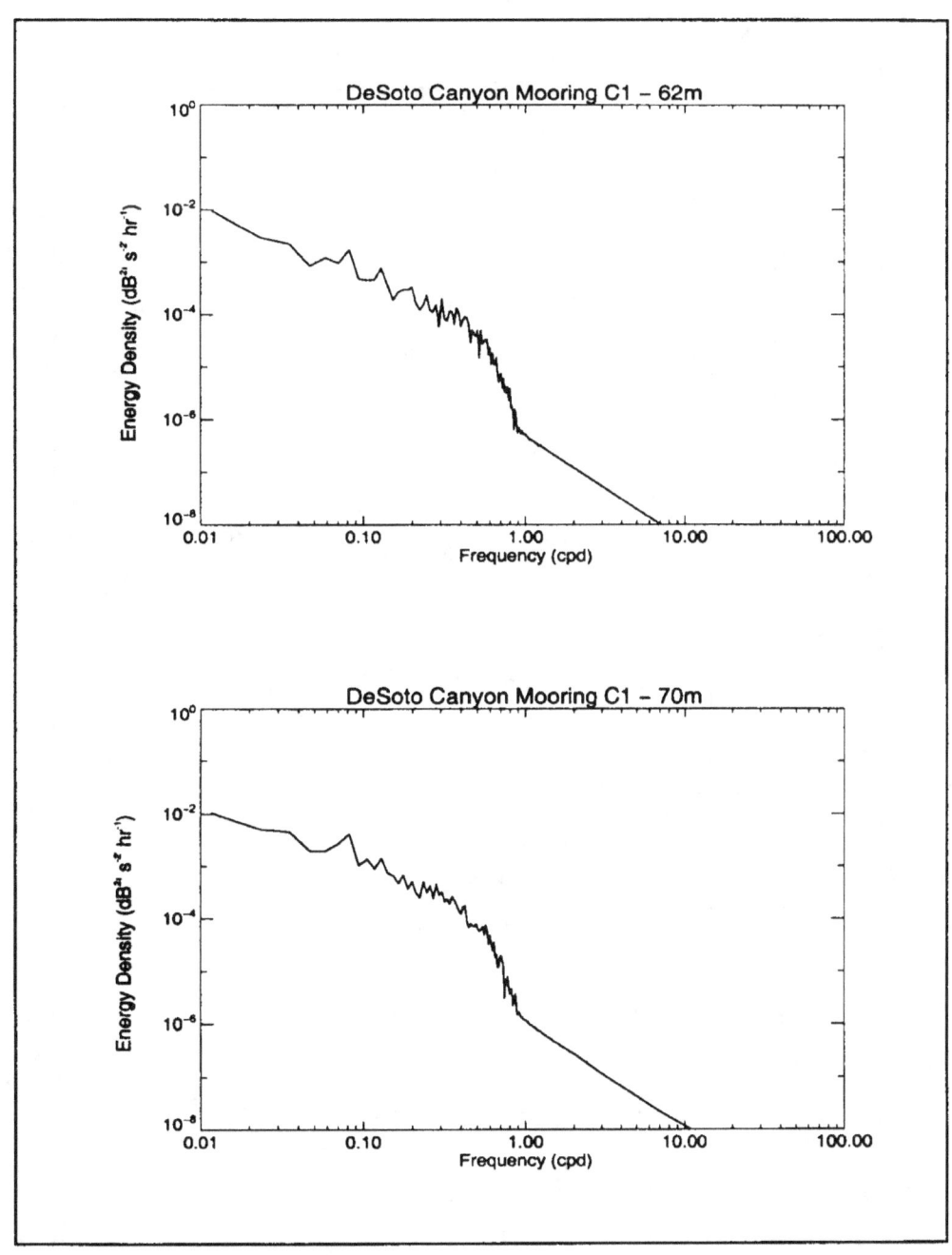

93

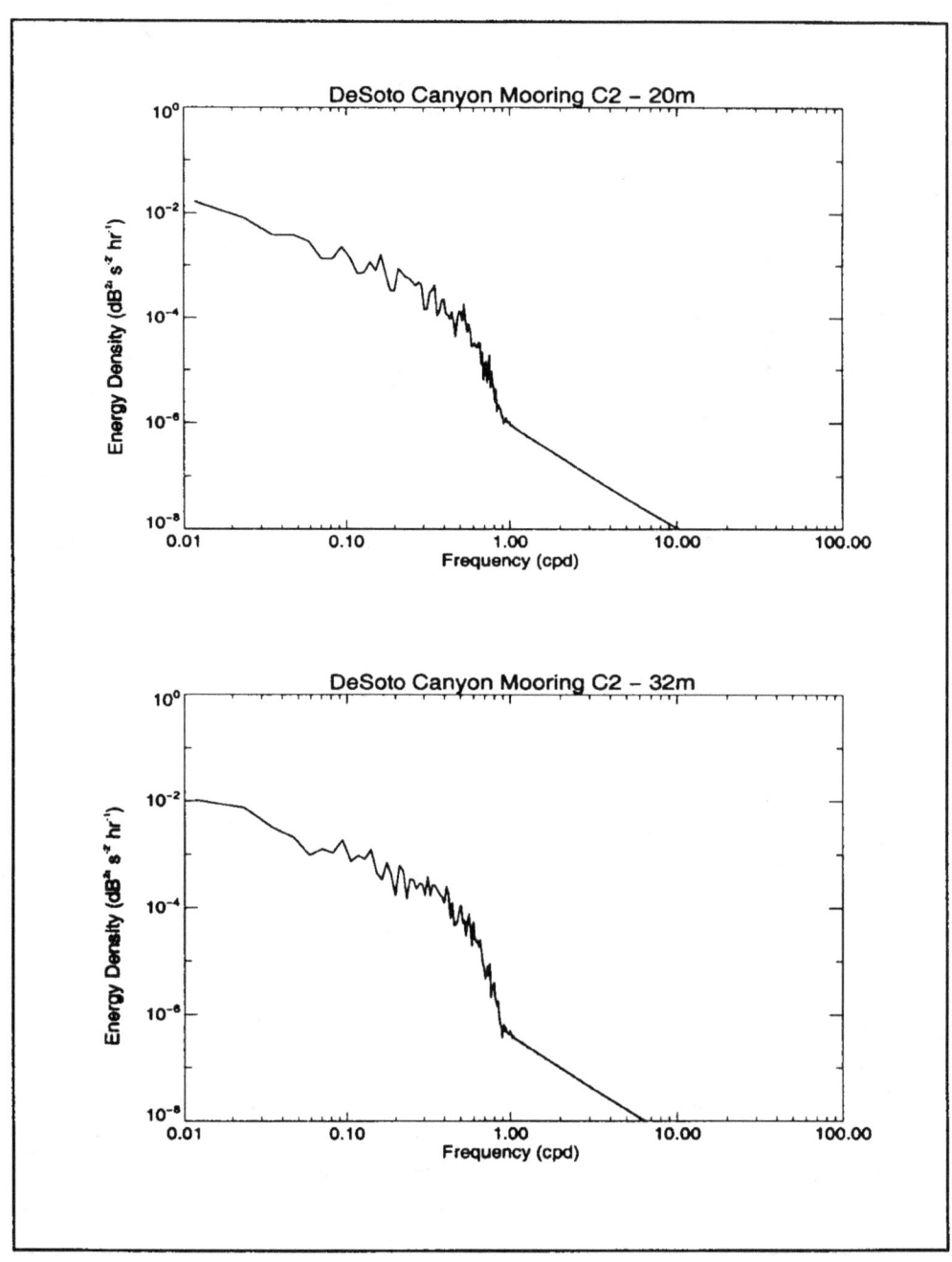

94

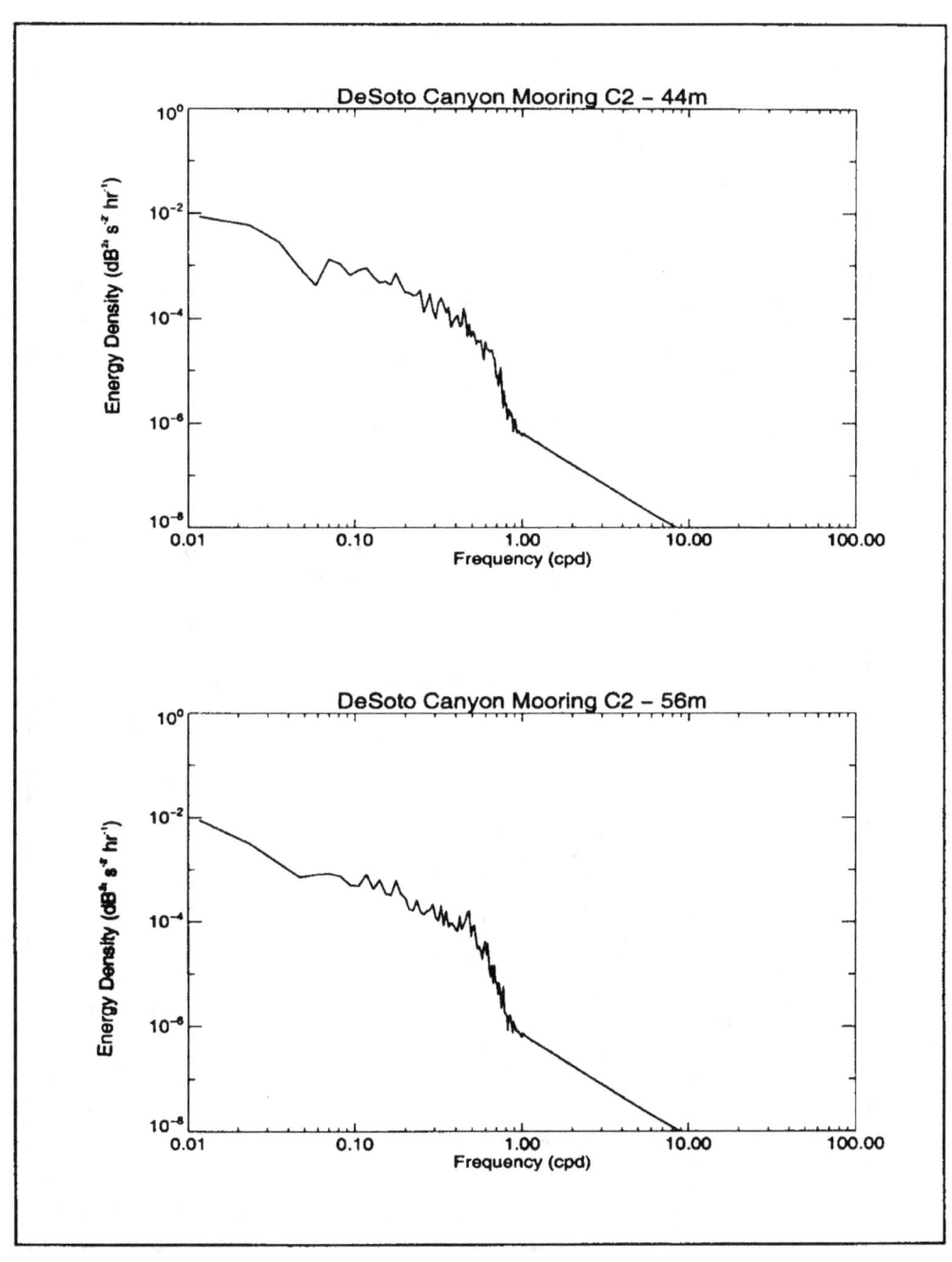

95

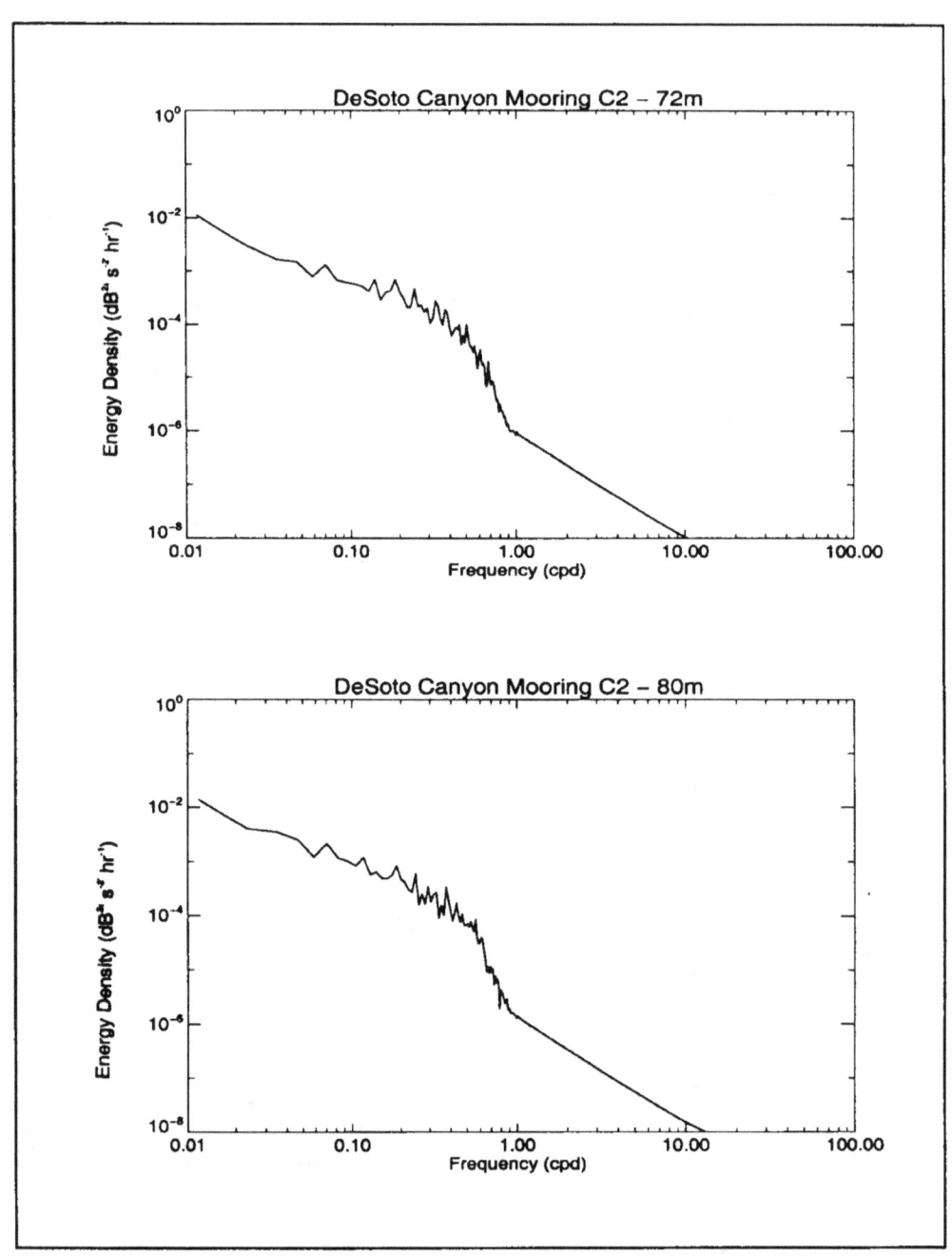

96

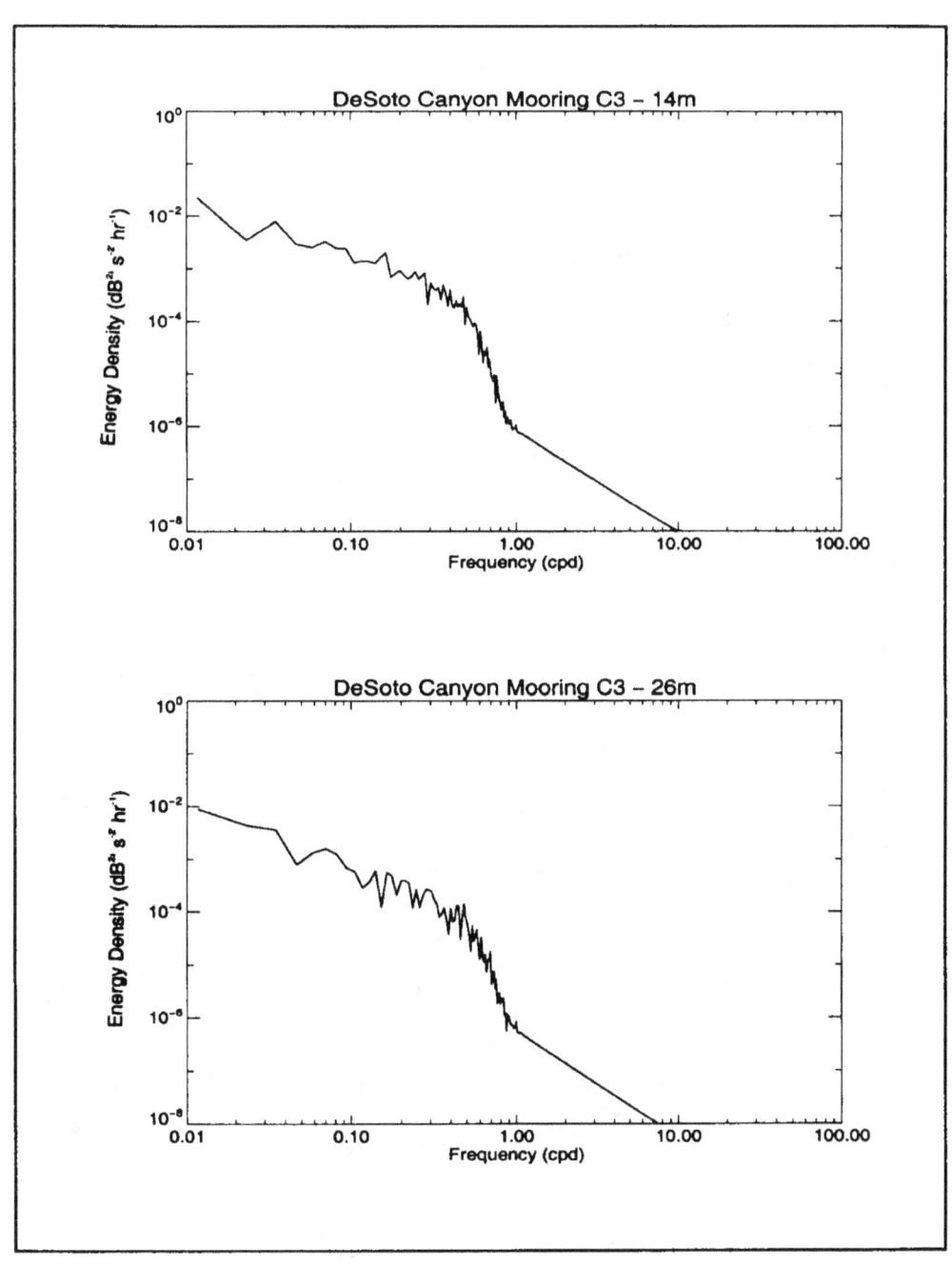

97

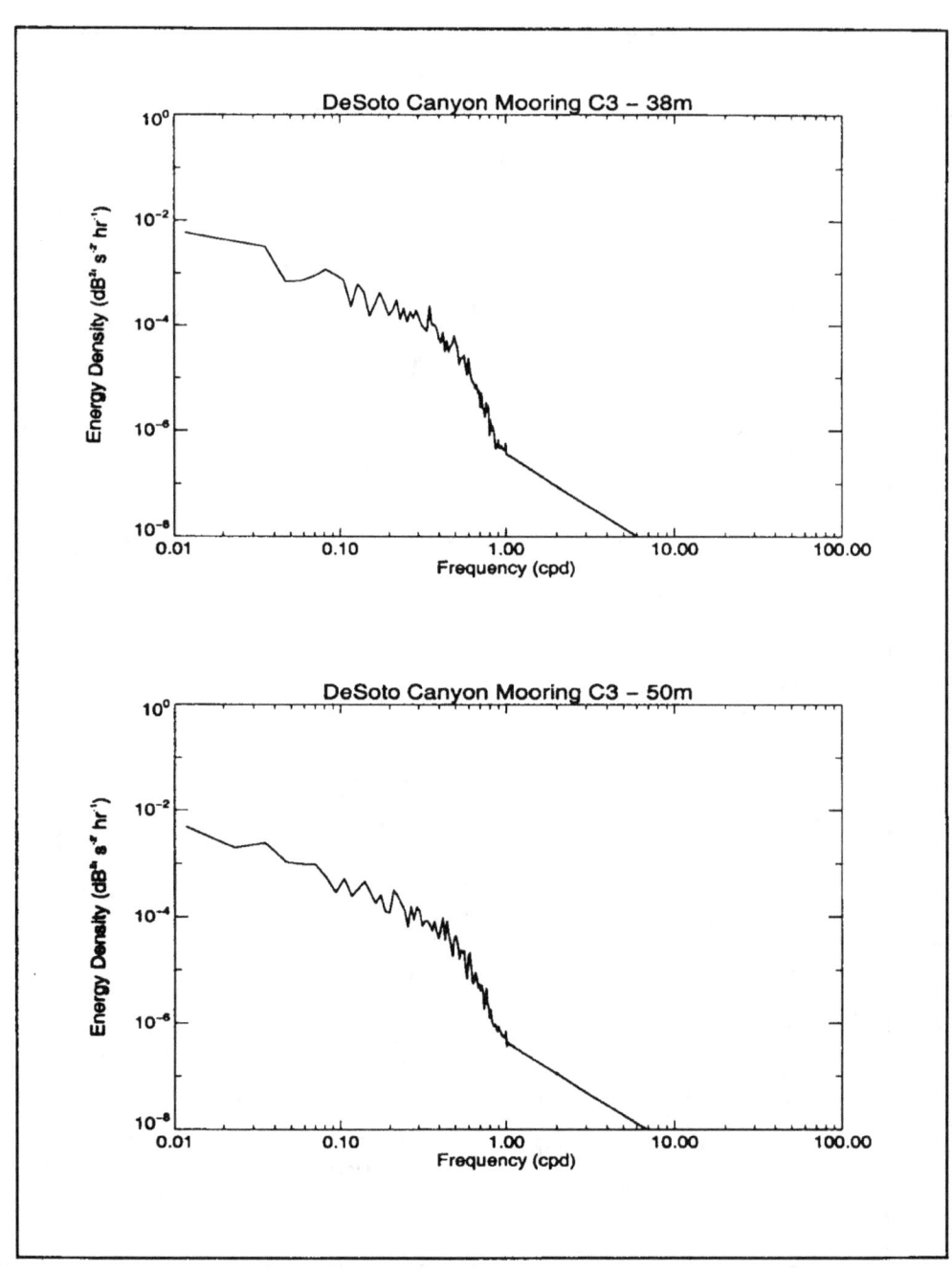

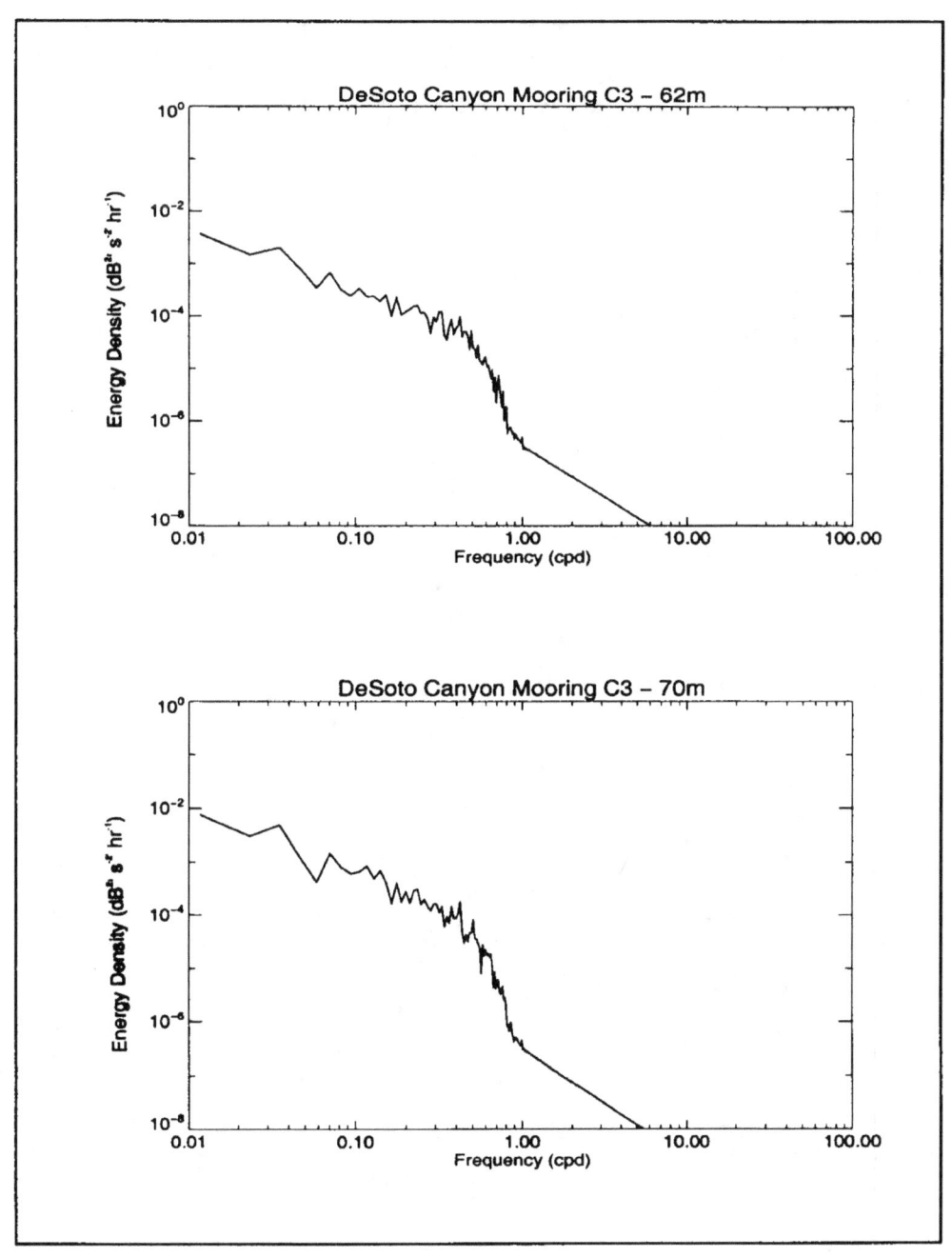

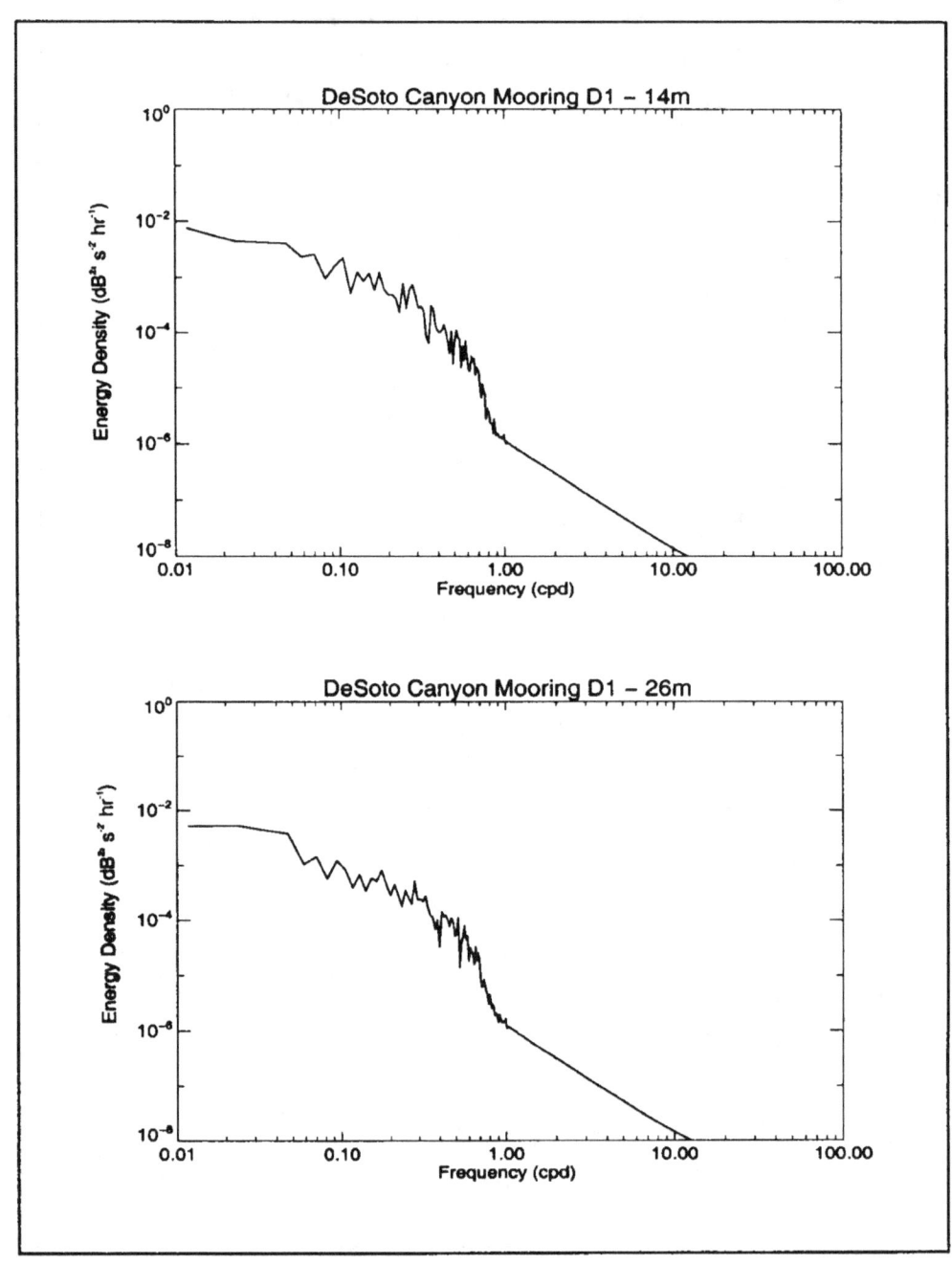

100

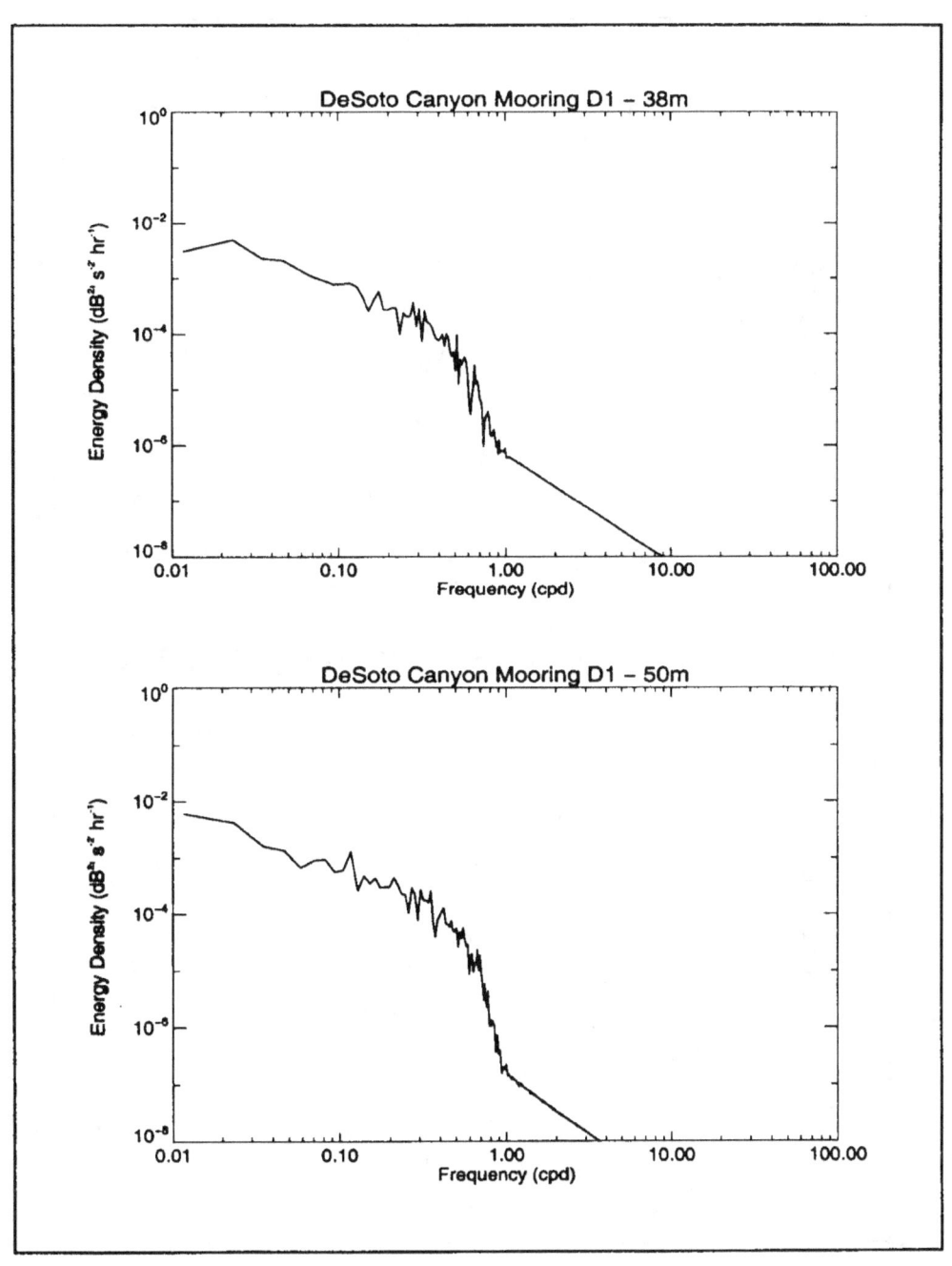

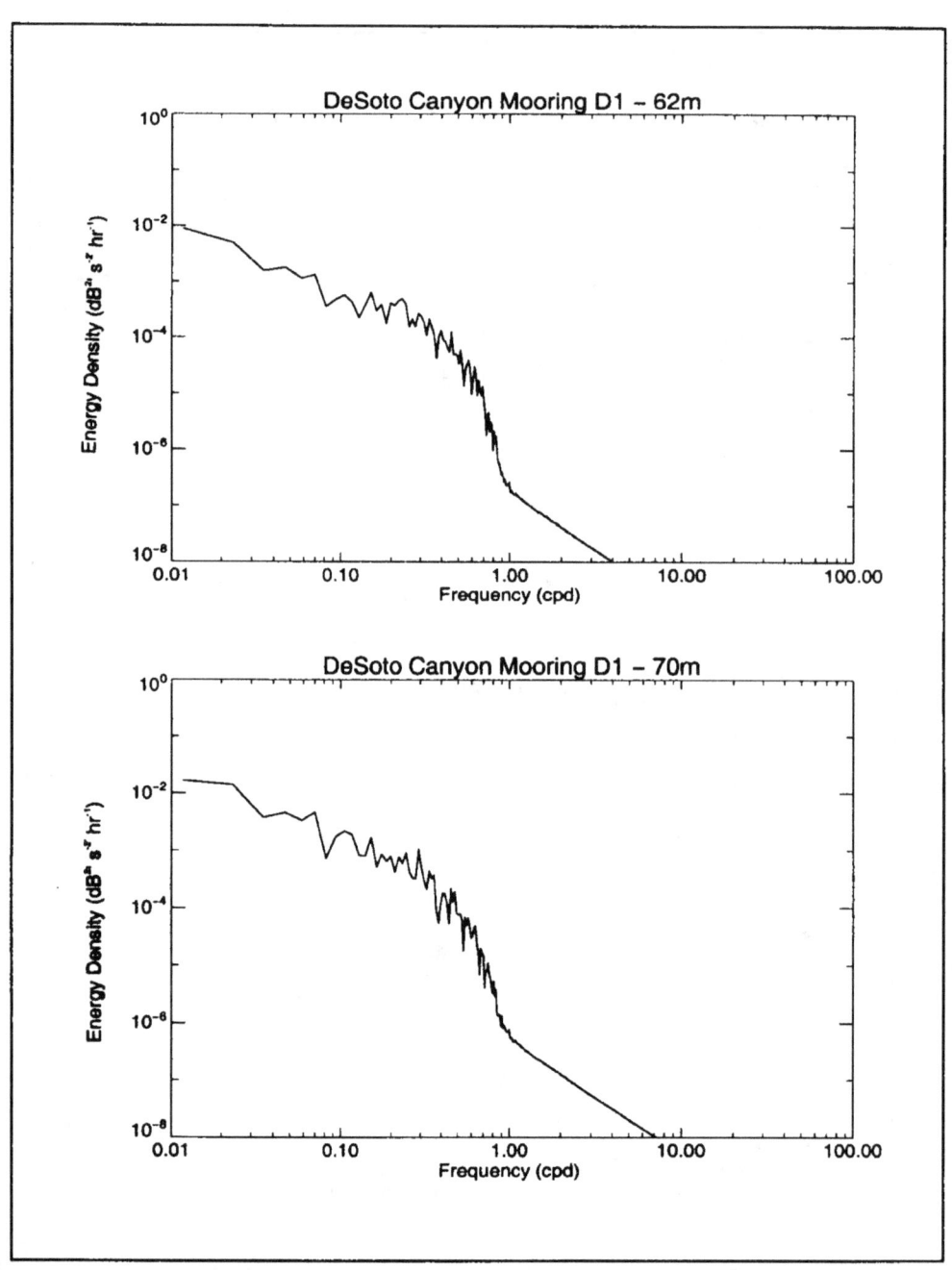

102

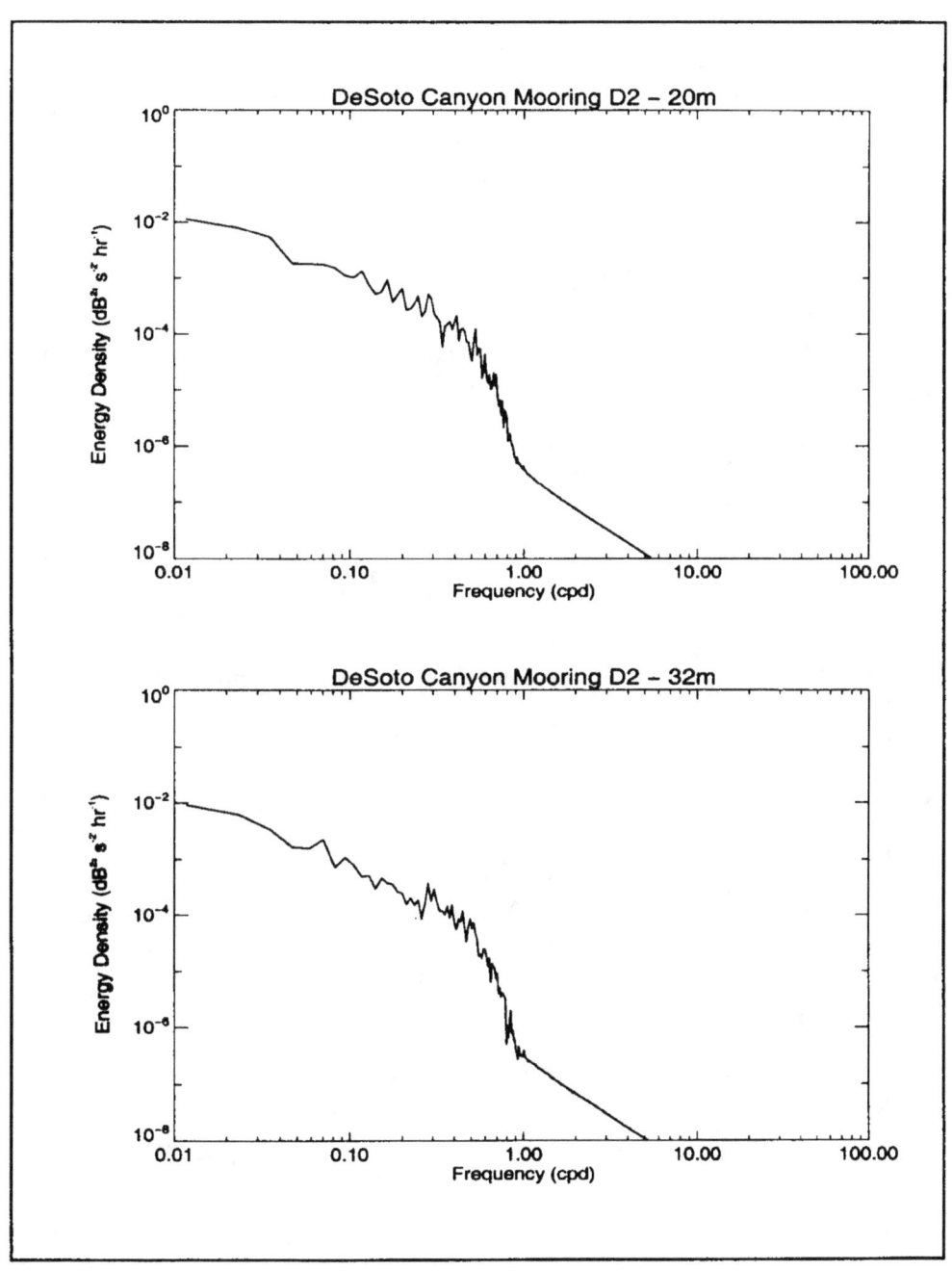

103

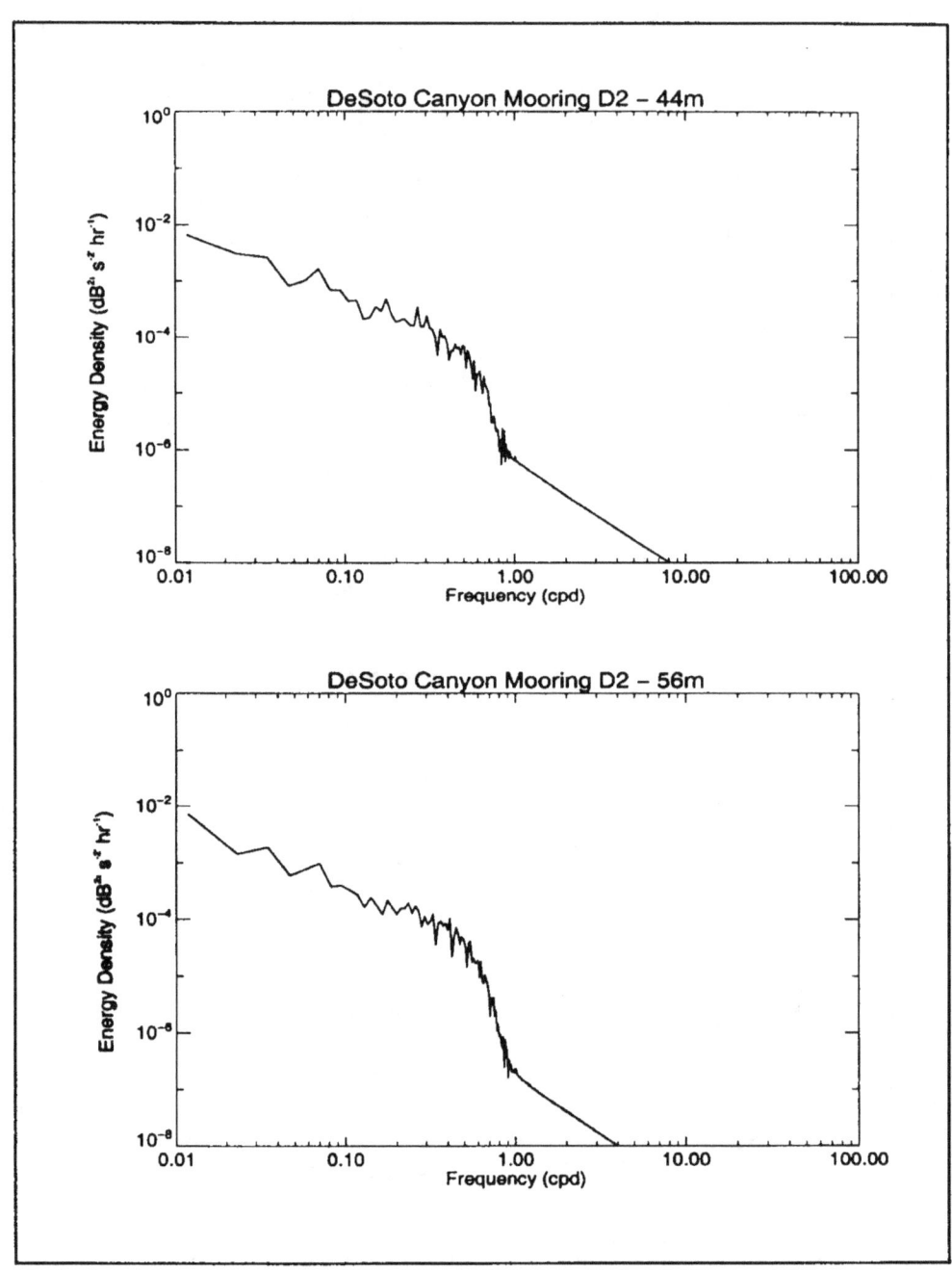

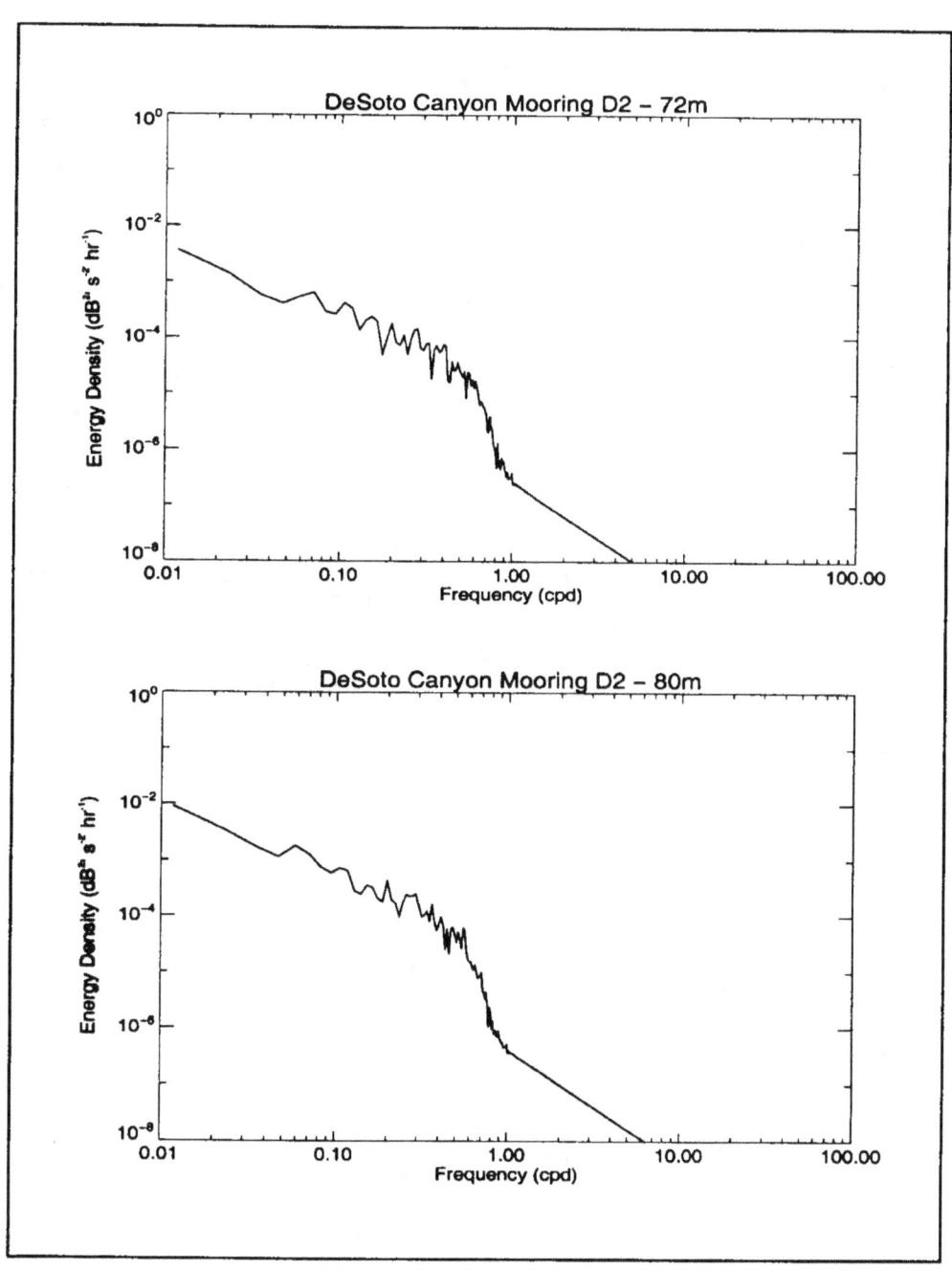

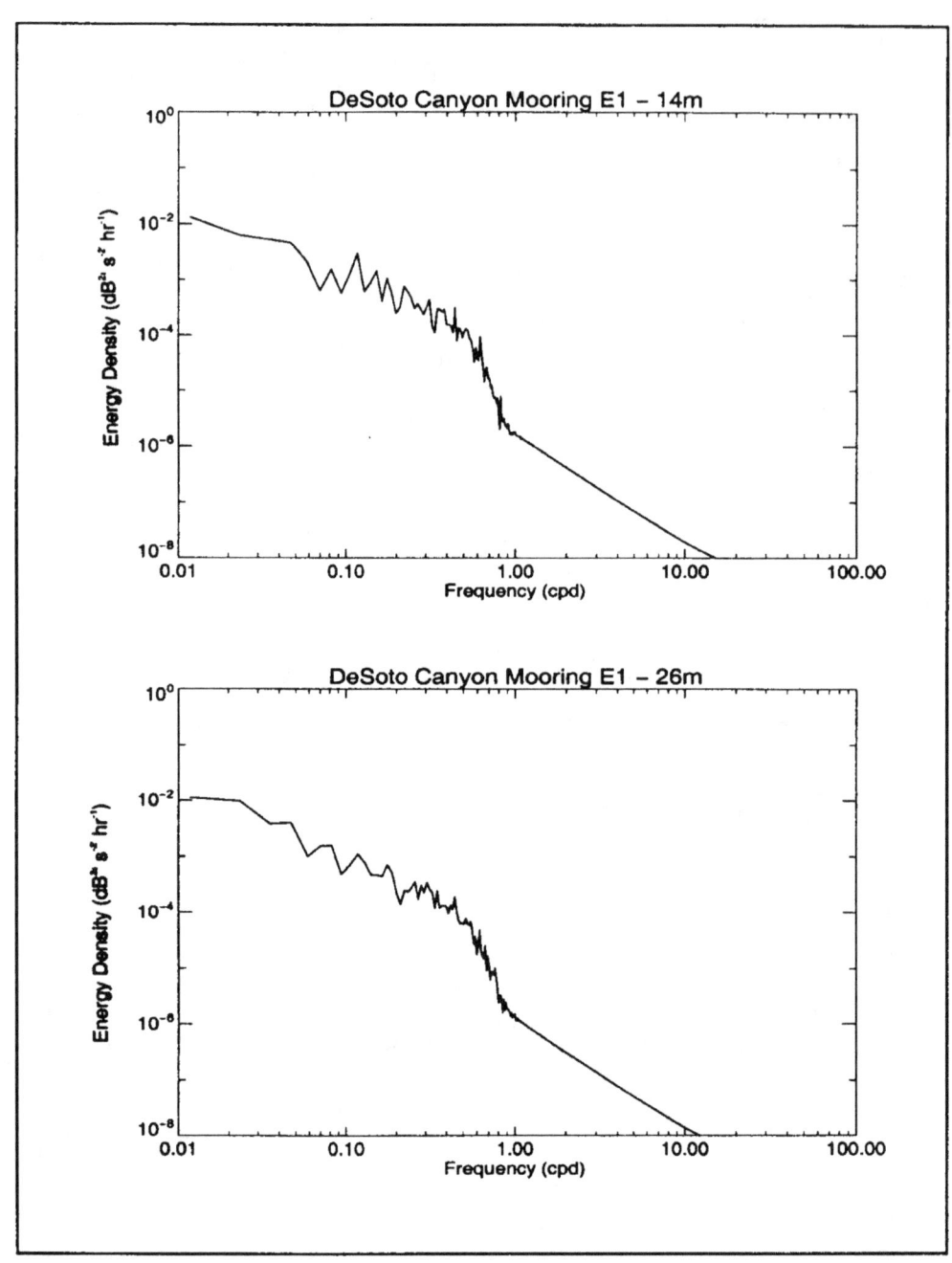

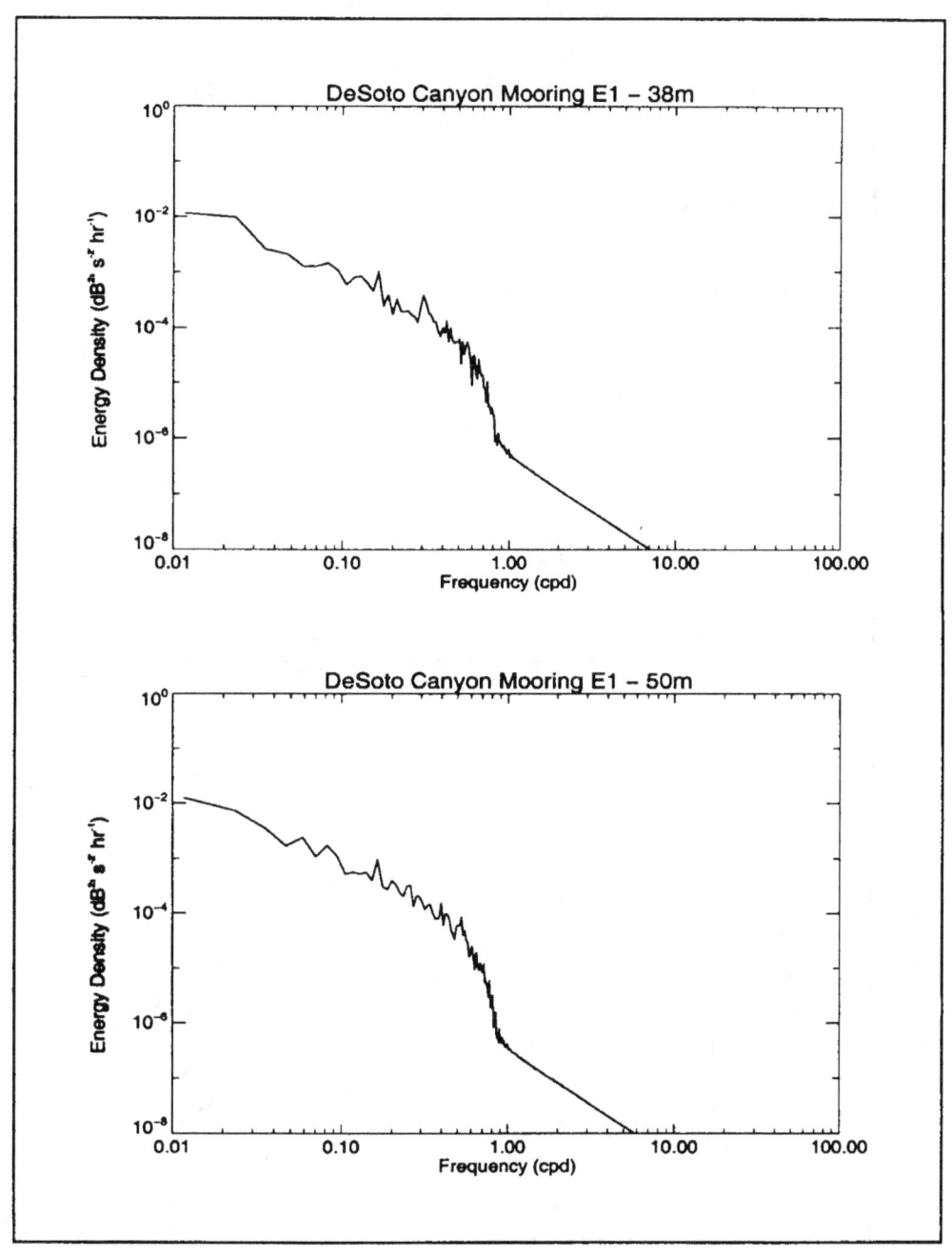

107

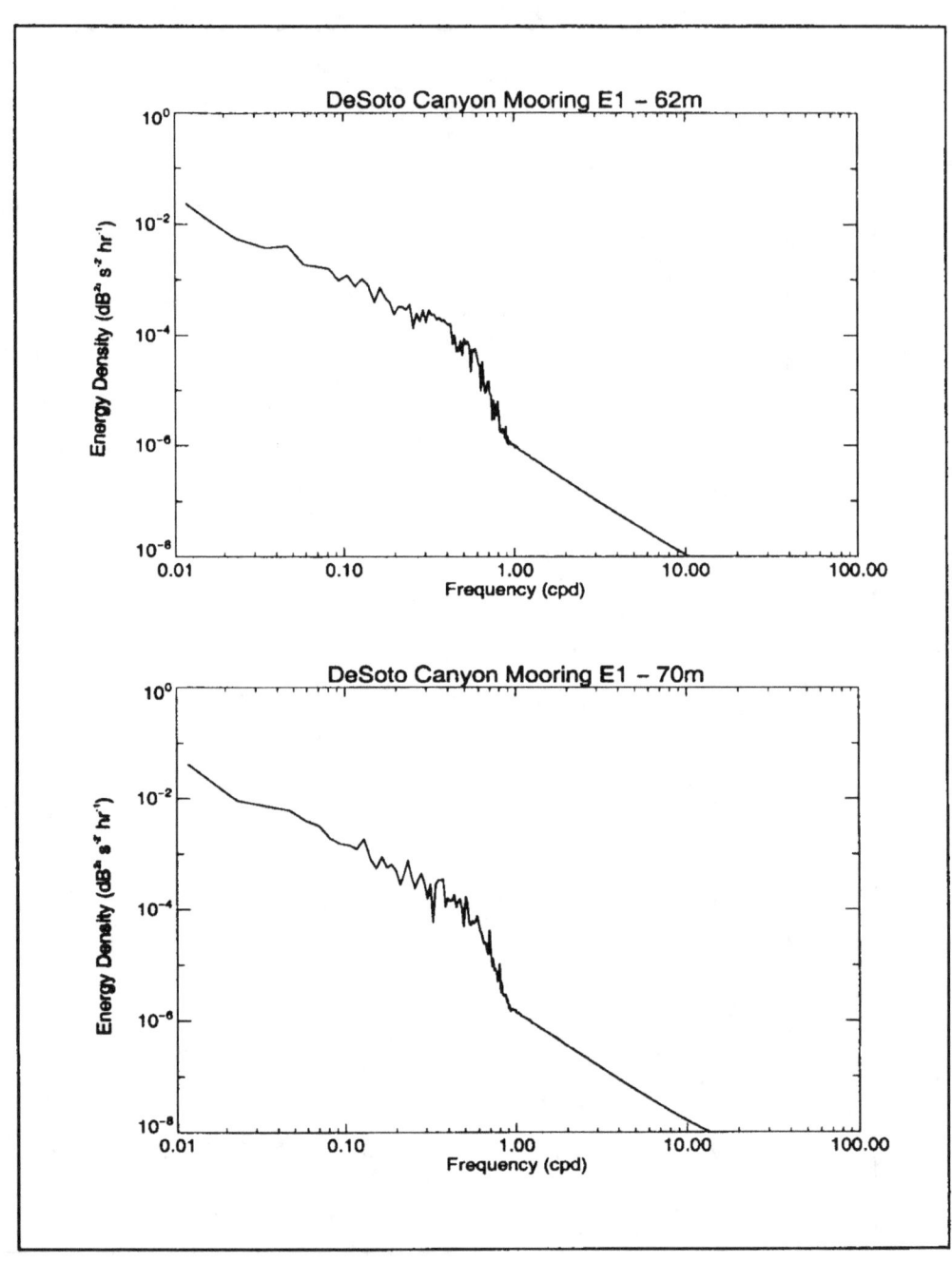

108

APPENDIX C:

**Rotated and 40-hour low-pass filtered current components
from one upper-water depth bin at six ADCP locations**

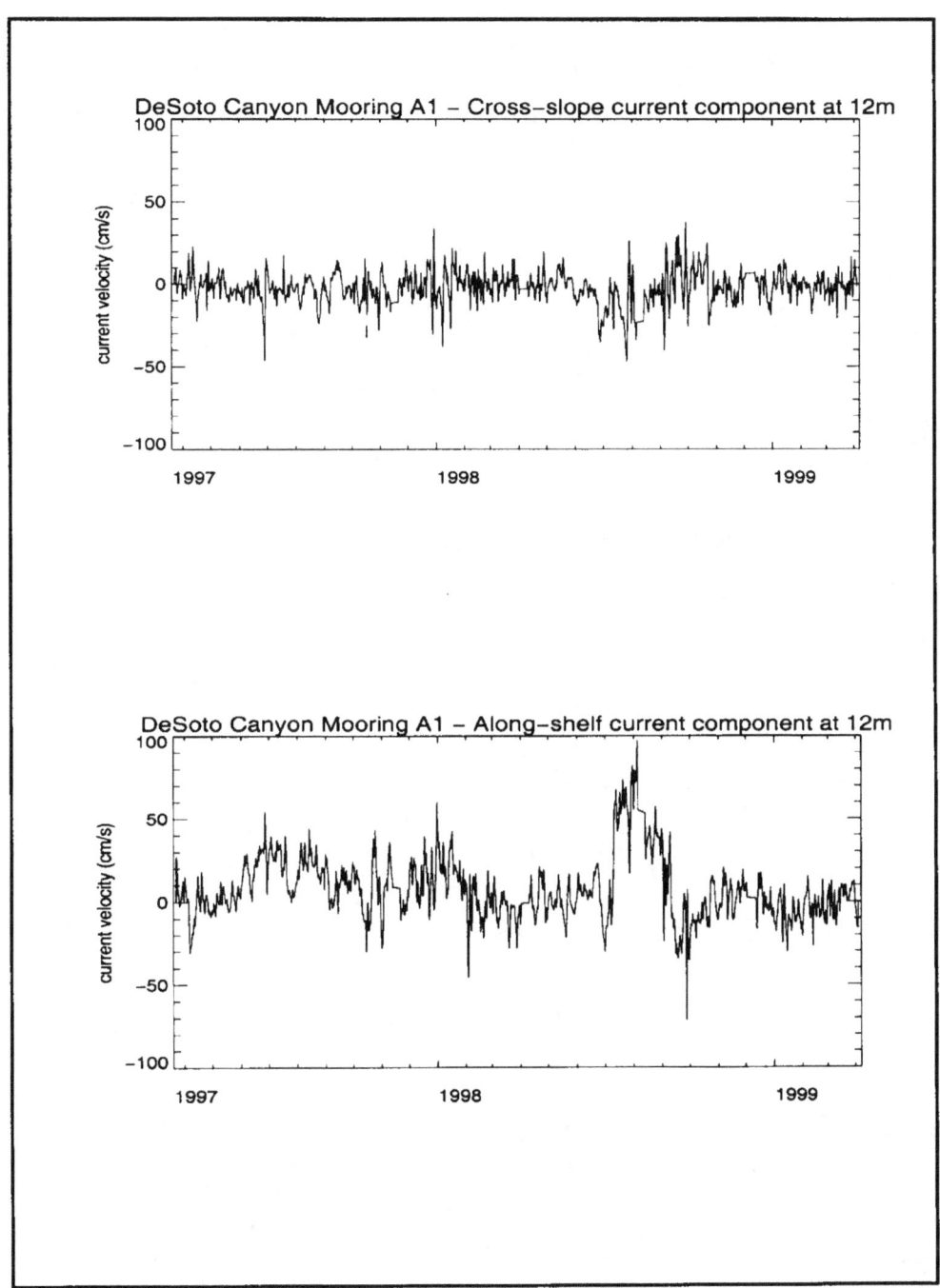

111

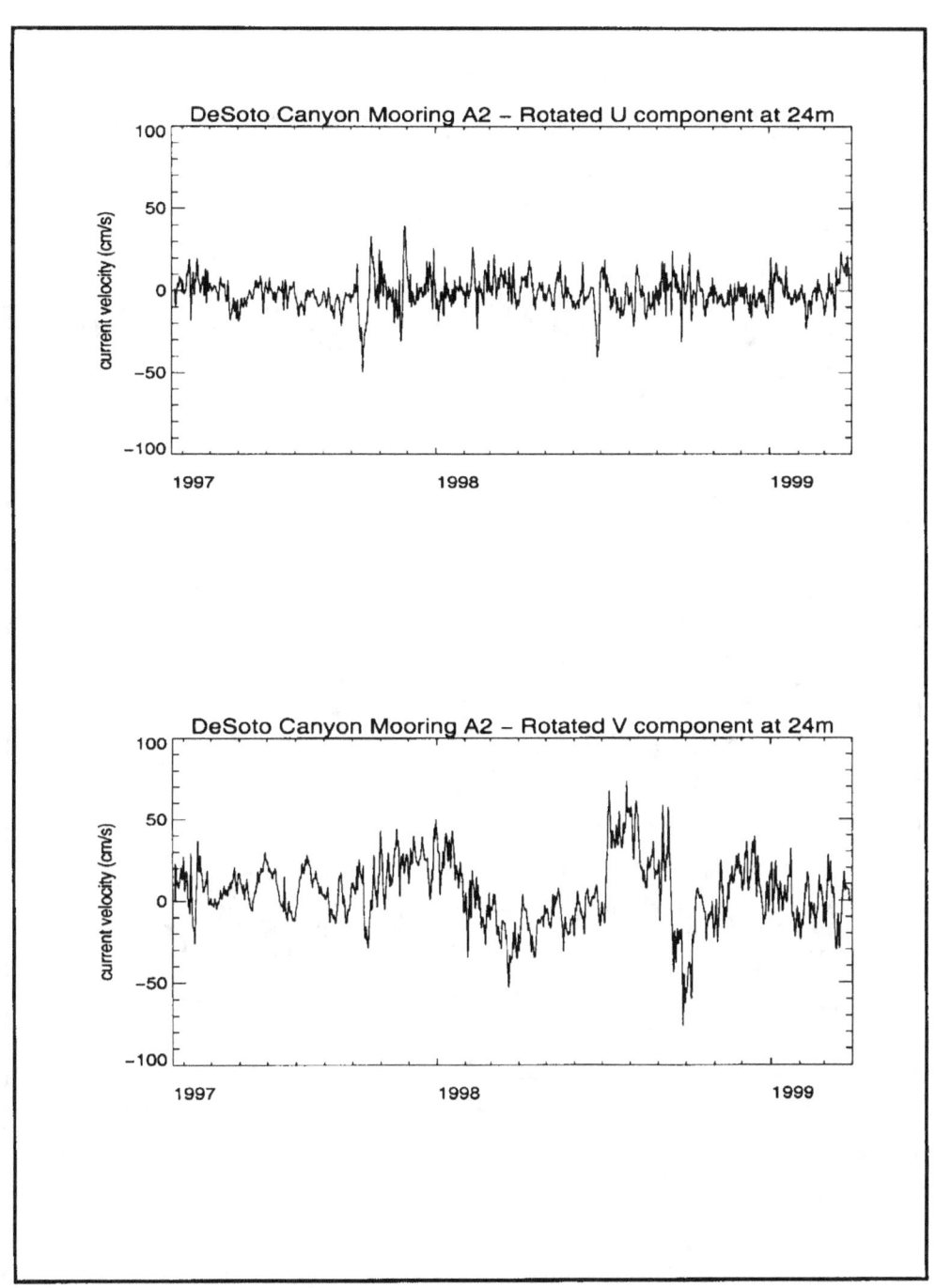

113

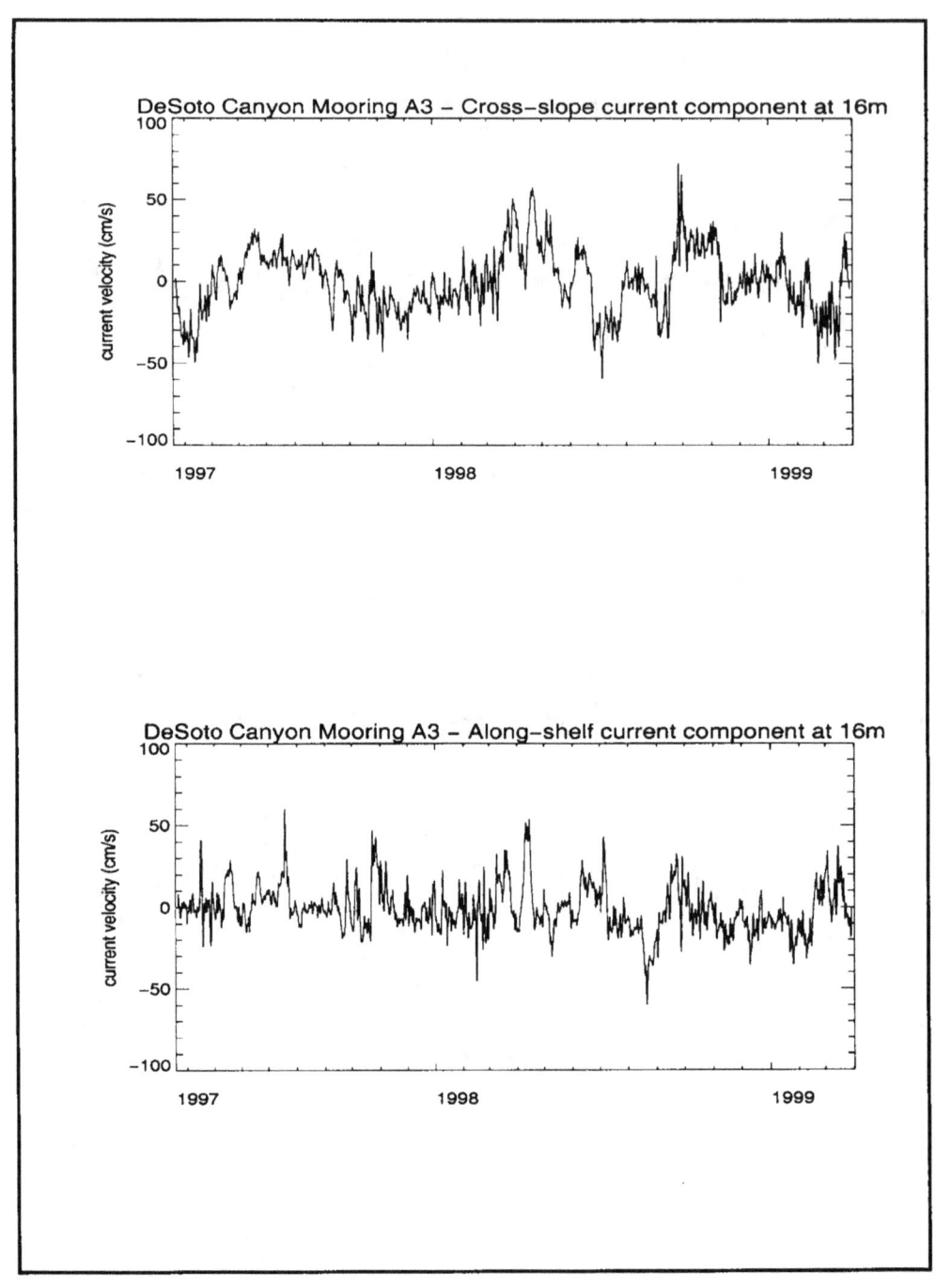

114

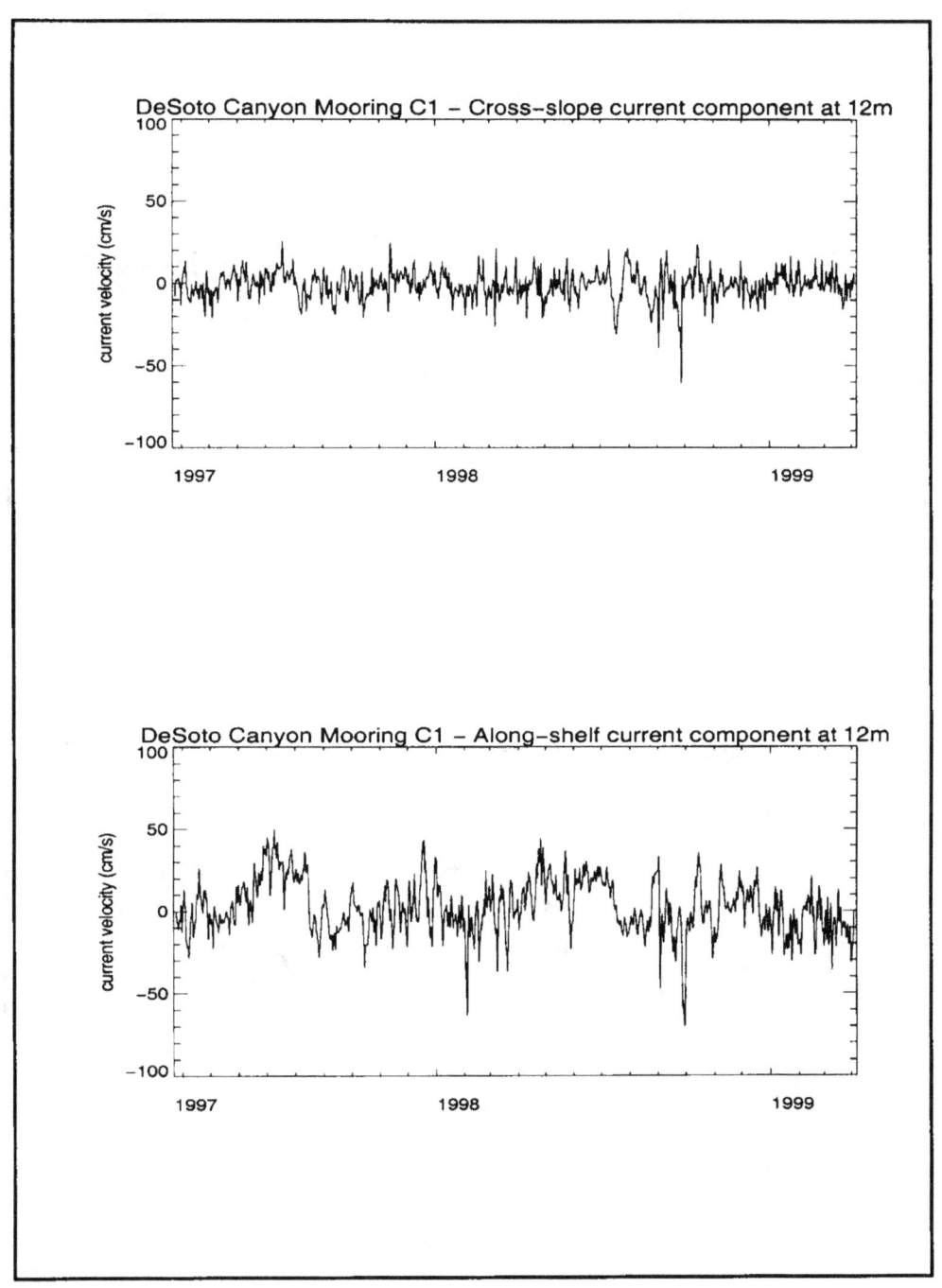

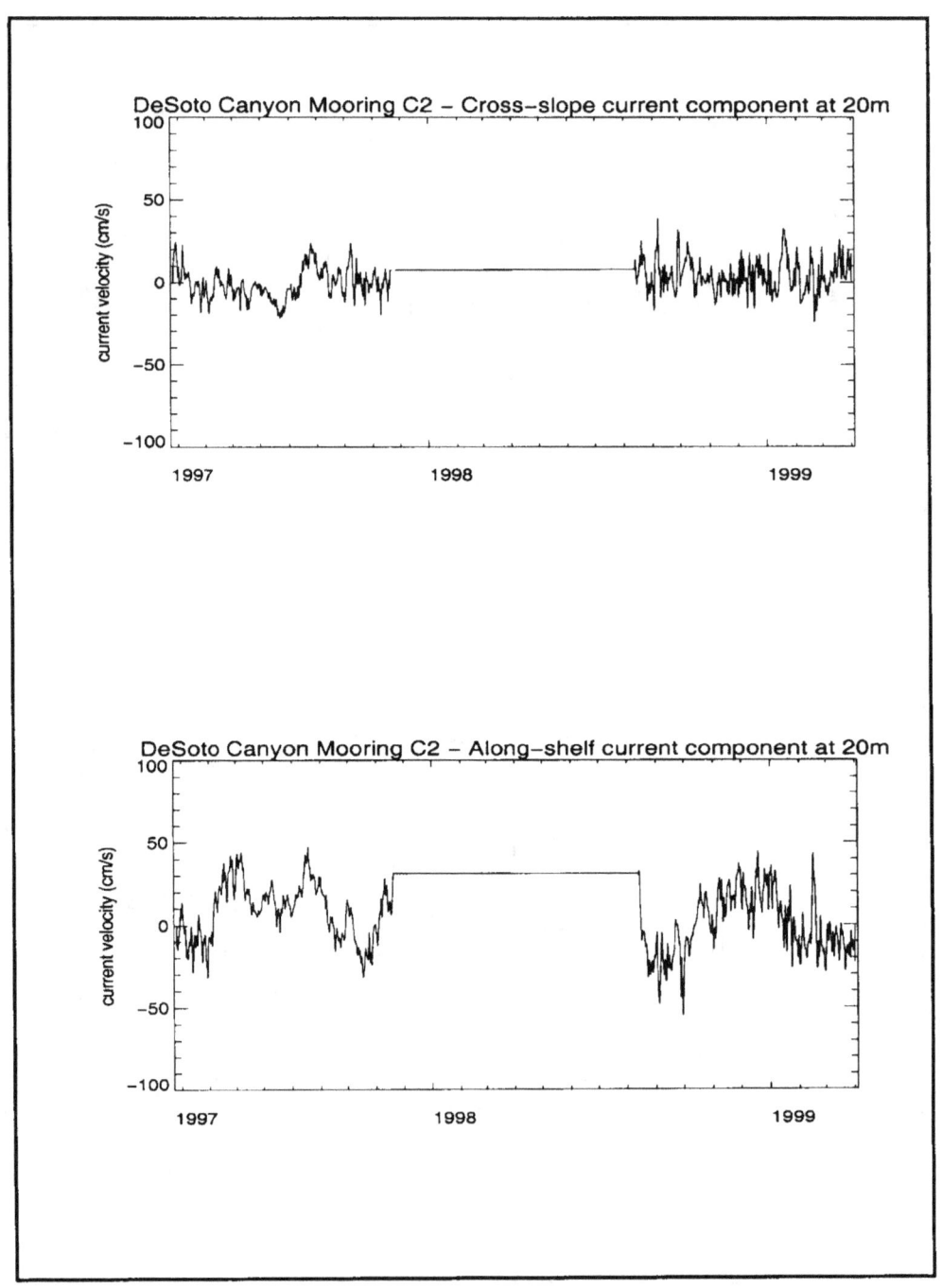

116

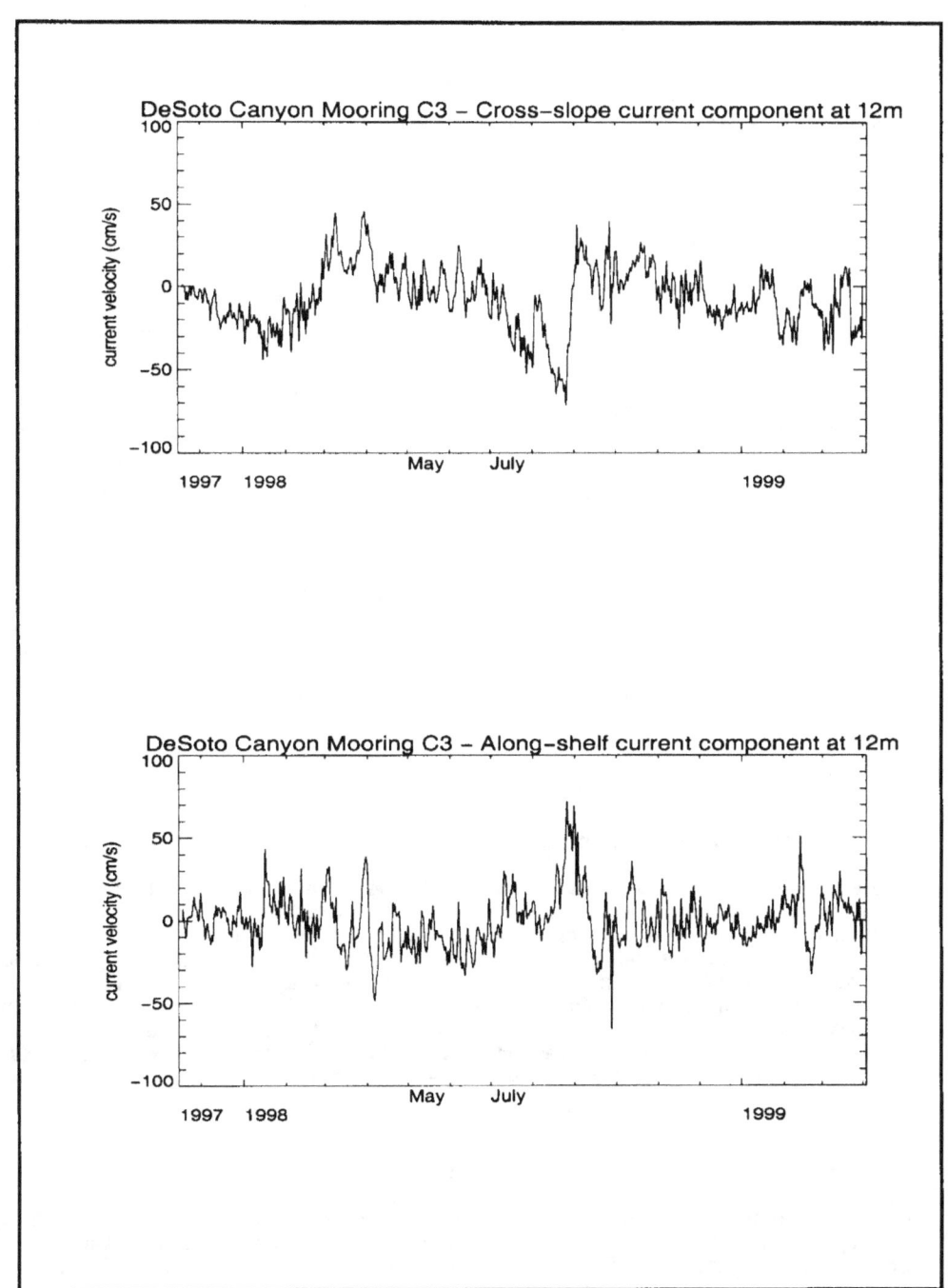

117

The Department of the Interior Mission

As the Nation's principal conservation agency, the Department of the Interior has responsibility for most of our nationally owned public lands and natural resources. This includes fostering sound use of our land and water resources; protecting our fish, wildlife, and biological diversity; preserving the environmental and cultural values of our national parks and historical places; and providing for the enjoyment of life through outdoor recreation. The Department assesses our energy and mineral resources and works to ensure that their development is in the best interests of all our people by encouraging stewardship and citizen participation in their care. The Department also has a major responsibility for American Indian reservation communities and for people who live in island territories under U.S. administration.

The Minerals Management Service Mission

As a bureau of the Department of the Interior, the Minerals Management Service's (MMS) primary responsibilities are to manage the mineral resources located on the Nation's Outer Continental Shelf (OCS), collect revenue from the Federal OCS and onshore Federal and Indian lands, and distribute those revenues.

Moreover, in working to meet its responsibilities, the **Offshore Minerals Management Program** administers the OCS competitive leasing program and oversees the safe and environmentally sound exploration and production of our Nation's offshore natural gas, oil and other mineral resources. The MMS **Minerals Revenue Management** meets its responsibilities by ensuring the efficient, timely and accurate collection and disbursement of revenue from mineral leasing and production due to Indian tribes and allottees, States and the U.S. Treasury.

The MMS strives to fulfill its responsibilities through the general guiding principles of: (1) being responsive to the public's concerns and interests by maintaining a dialogue with all potentially affected parties and (2) carrying out its programs with an emphasis on working to enhance the quality of life for all Americans by lending MMS assistance and expertise to economic development and environmental protection.